Trading Spaces™

TRIVIA

Seasons 1 through 3

D1444060

Meredith® Books
Des Moines, Iowa

Trading Spaces Trivia
Editor: Amy Tincher-Durik
Senior Associate Design Director: Ken Carlson
Writer: Kellie Kramer
Copy Chief: Terri Fredrickson
Copy and Production Editor: Victoria Forlini
Editorial Operations Manager: Karen Schirm
Managers, Book Production: Pam Kvitne, Marjorie J.
  Schenkelberg, Rick von Holdt
Contributing Proofreaders: Sara Henderson, Gretchen Kauffman,
  Jeanée Ledoux
Editorial and Design Assistants: Kaye Chabot, Karen McFadden,
  Mary Lee Gavin

Meredith Books
Editor in Chief: Linda Raglan Cunningham
Design Director: Matt Strelecki
Executive Editor, Home Decorating and Design: Denise L. Caringer

Publisher: James D. Blume
Executive Director, Marketing: Jeffrey Myers
Executive Director, New Business Development: Todd M. Davis
Executive Director, Sales: Ken Zagor
Director, Operations: George A. Susral
Director, Production: Douglas M. Johnston
Business Director: Jim Leonard

Vice President and General Manager: Douglas J. Guendel

Meredith Publishing Group
President, Publishing Group: Stephen M. Lacy
Vice President-Publishing Director: Bob Mate

Meredith Corporation
Chairman and Chief Executive Officer: William T. Kerr

In Memoriam: E. T. Meredith III (1933–2003)

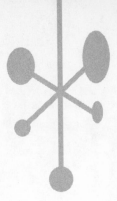

All of us at Meredith Books are dedicated to providing you with
information and ideas to enhance your home. We welcome your
comments and suggestions. Write to us at: Meredith Books, Home
Decorating and Design Editorial Department, 1716 Locust St., Des
Moines, IA 50309-3023.

If you would like to purchase any of our home decorating and
design, cooking, crafts, gardening, or home improvement books,
check wherever quality books are sold.
Or visit us at: meredithbooks.com

All questions included in this book are based on Seasons 1 to 3 of
Trading Spaces. All efforts have been made to ensure answers are
correct as of time of printing.

TLC (The Learning Channel), TLC (The
Learning Channel) logo, Trading Spaces,
and the Trading Spaces logo are
trademarks of Discovery Communications,
Inc., used under license.
Trading Spaces **Book Development Team**
Kathy Davidov, Executive Producer, TLC
Roger Marmet, General Manager, TLC
Tom Farrell, Executive Producer, Banyan
Productions
Sharon M. Bennett, Senior Vice President,
Strategic Partnerships & Licensing
Carol LeBlanc, Vice President, Marketing &
Retail Development
Dee Scott, Vice President, Licensing
Erica Jacobs Green, Publishing Manager
Elizabeth Bakacs, Creative Director,
Strategic Partnerships

contents

Whether you've seen a few episodes—or all 144—this book is sure to test your knowledge of everything that makes this decorating show unique. Get ready for the ultimate *Trading Spaces* challenge!

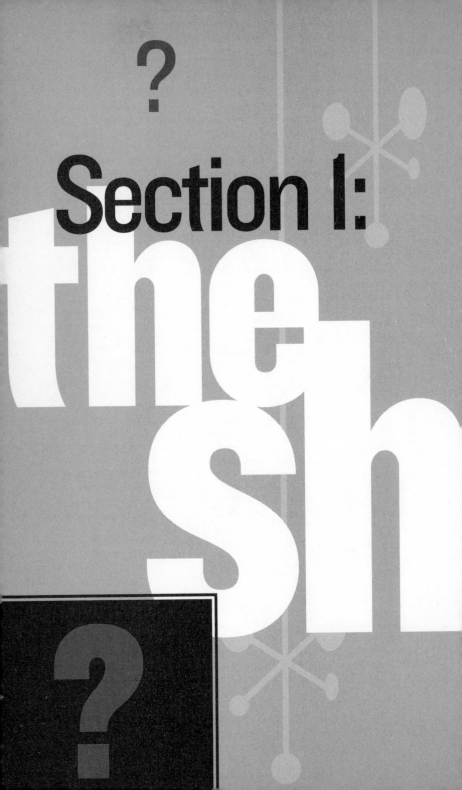

?

Section I:

the

sh

Sure, you're a *Trading Spaces* fan—you know the cast members' birthdates and hum the show's theme music in the shower—but what do you know about the making of the show and its history?

OW?

1 carpenter   4 friends
$1,000 budget
2 designers

1. **TLC's slogan is:**
   a. Life Unscripted
   b. Life Unscheduled
   c. Life Unrehearsed
   d. Life Undefined

2. *Trading Spaces* airs on TLC _____ times per week.

3. **What have homeowners not held during the Key Swap?**
   a. an espresso machine
   b. a personal massager
   c. a teddy bear
   d. a blender

4. **True or False? There are three Season 3 pillows.**

5. **Which *Trading Spaces* logo item is not available for sale on the TLC website?**
   a. tool belt
   b. coffee mug
   c. lunch sack
   d. journal

6. **In order to qualify for *Trading Spaces*, the neighbors' homes cannot be more than a _____ minute walk apart.**

The *Trading Spaces* bulletin board at tlc.discovery.com gets more than 750,000 page views per month.

7. **True or False? Everyone on camera wears the same clothes both days to assist in the editing process.**

8. **Members of the *Trading Spaces* cast transformed offices on which morning news/talk show?**
   a. *The Early Show*
   b. *Good Morning America*
   c. *Today Show*
   d. *Fox & Friends*

Answers begin on page 12

9. *Trading Spaces* receives approximately _____ online applications daily from prospective homeowners.

10. True or False? *Trading Spaces* was the only cable show nominated in its category at the 2002 Primetime Emmy Awards.

11. *Trading Spaces* is currently produced by:
a. Ross Communications
b. The Learning Channel
c. Banyan Productions
d. Discovery Communications, Inc.

Trading Spaces has filmed 22 episodes in California, more than any other state.

12. The area where Amy Wynn, Ty, and Carter create wonderful carpentry pieces is commonly referred to as:
a. Carpentry-Verse
b. Carpentry Land
c. Carpentry Country
d. Carpentry World

13. For the duration of filming, homeowners are specifically asked to make other arrangements for their:
a. vehicles and deliveries
b. kids and pets
c. vehicles and kids
d. pets and deliveries

14. True or False? Homeowners are occasionally allowed to choose their designer.

15. True or False? Filming on Day One begins bright and early at 5:30 a.m.

16. True or False? Despite the name, PaigeCam footage is actually filmed by a trained camera operator.

17. Model/Actress Rebecca Romijn-Stamos told Jay Leno in an interview that she watches *Trading Spaces* so often she's shortened the name to _____.

18. The shots of the cast "hamming it up" at a site near where an episode is filmed at the start of an episode is called:

a. B-roll
b. P-roll
c. V-roll
d. D-roll

19. Which of *Trading Spaces'* fellow nominees won the statue at the 2002 Primetime Emmy Awards?

a. *AFI's 100 Years… 100 Thrills, America's Most Heart Pounding Movies* (CBS)
b. *I Love Lucy 50th Anniversary Special* (CBS)
c. *The West Wing Documentary Special* (NBC)
d. *Survivor* (CBS)

20. True or False? The overhead camera mounted in each room is running throughout the entire two-day process, and the footage that isn't needed is edited out.

Trading Spaces online receives an average of 14 million hits per month.

21. True or False? The $1,000-per-room budget includes everything from lumber to paintbrushes.

22. _____ assists Ty, Amy Wynn, and Carter with their carpentry projects.

23. _____ is the only homeowner who has handpicked his/her designer.

24. In order to receive a makeover on the show, a room's dimensions must be at least:

a. 10'x12'
b. 14'x14'
c. 12'x14'
d. 12'x12'

25. True or False? An episode of *Trading Spaces* is taped over the course of three days.

26. TLC airs a popular *Trading Spaces* marathon on _____.

> *Trading Spaces* is TLC's No. 1 regularly scheduled program.

27. To prepare for an episode, designers typically have:
   a. one to two months
   b. three to four days
   c. two to three weeks
   d. five to six hours

28. In 2002, *Trading Spaces* was nominated for a Primetime Emmy in the _____ category.

29. TLC has released three *Trading Spaces* DVDs called: _____.

30. The show's producers, Banyan Productions, are based out of _____.

31. True or False? Although rebroadcasts can be caught several times per week, new episodes of *Trading Spaces* premiere at 8 p.m. and 9 p.m. ET/PT Saturday nights.

01:40:09.16

Who designed this room?

32. To congratulate and thank them for their 2002 Emmy nomination, TLC presented the *Trading Spaces* cast and crew with:

    a. a large cake
    b. logo baseball hats
    c. commemorative pen sets
    d. matching show jackets

33. TLC's parent company is _____.

34. The animated images between Days One and Two are referred to as the _____.

35. The late night talk show that spoofed *Trading Spaces* by having soldiers redo each other's tents in bright colors was:

    a. *Late Night with Conan O'Brien*
    b. *The Tonight Show with Jay Leno*
    c. *The Late Show with David Letterman*
    d. *The Daily Show with John Stewart*

Trading Spaces averages more than 6 million viewers per week.

36. True or False? When a designer goes over budget, the extra cash comes from a production budget specifically set up to cover overruns.

37. True or False? Although a small trailer is seen on camera, the *Trading Spaces* equipment travels from location to location in a semitruck.

38. The sped-up footage of items being carried in and out of a room is called:

    a. Load Out and Load In
    b. Move Out and Move In
    c. Lug Out and Lug In
    d. Throw Out and Bring In

39. The short shots shown before and after commercials are called:

    a. bumpers
    b. cappers
    c. toppers
    d. stingers

40. *Trading Spaces* is based on the BBC show _____.

41. The only brand of sewing machine the cast and crew use during the filming of any episode is:
   a. Singer
   b. Brother
   c. Bernina
   d. Simplicity

42. True or False? Furniture from the room being redecorated is stored anywhere there's an open space in the home.

43. True or False? Designers often watch The Reveal from nearby on a monitor.

44. The color of the *Trading Spaces* smock that was discontinued early in the run of the show is:
   a. yellow
   b. black
   c. orange
   d. purple

45. True or False? The show's crew includes a makeup artist and a costumer.

46. A _____ appears in each Season 3 episode with the roman numeral III on it.

47. The first day of taping in a location is called _____.

48. True or False? Homeowners are not allowed in the house while the Designer Chat is filmed.

49. The four colors of *Trading Spaces* smocks currently worn by homeowners are _____.

50. Sewing World, the home of the show's sewing projects, is often found in what location during filming?
   a. the *Trading Spaces* trailer
   b. one of the homeowners' garages
   c. one of the homeowners' patios
   d. one of the homeowners' driveways

Section I: Answers

1. **A.** Life Unscripted

2. **eight**

3. **B.** a personal massager

4. **False.** There are two: one light and one dark.

5. **A.** tool belt

6. **two**

7. **True.** While there is some obvious continuity, smaller segments like sewing or craft projects are edited in wherever it makes the most sense regardless of the day they were actually filmed.

8. **C.** *Today Show*

9. **300 to 500**

10. **True.** The competition came from CBS and NBC.

11. **C.** Banyan Productions

12. **D.** Carpentry World

13. **B.** kids and pets

14. **False.** While homeowners are allowed to state their preferences, they have no say in the final decision.

15. **False.** Taping usually begins around 8 a.m., with the Key Swap being filmed at 9 a.m.

16. **False.** Paige lugs a personal video camera from house to house, capturing unexpected moments as she sees fit.

17. *Tray Spay*

18. **A.** B-roll

19. **C.** *The West Wing Documentary Special* (NBC)

20. **False.** The "overhead" is started and stopped at various points during the process—sometimes by the designers as they work late into the night after the camera crew has left for the day.

21. **False.** General supplies like sandpaper and paintbrushes aren't included.

22. **"Fast" Eddie Barnard**

23. **Natalie Maines, lead singer of the Dixie Chicks**

24. **B.** 14'x14'

25. **True.** The first day, Day Zero, is a day for shopping and taping B-roll. Days One and Two are for redecorating the rooms.

26. **Memorial Day**

27. **C.** two to three weeks

28. **Outstanding Special Class Program**

29. *The Best of Trading Spaces, Trading Spaces: They Hated It!, Trading Spaces: Viewers' Choice*

30. **Philadelphia, Pennsylvania**

31. **False.** New episodes of *Trading Spaces* premiere on Saturday nights at 9 p.m., but previously aired episodes are repeated at 8 p.m.

32. **D.** matching show jackets

33. **Discovery Communications, Inc.**

34. **Day to Night Graphic**

35. **A.** *Late Night with Conan O'Brien*

36. **False.** Anything after the initial $1,000 budget comes out of the designers' pockets.

37. **False.** What you see on camera is all there is: a small trailer hauled by a GMC 4x4 truck.

38. A. Load Out and Load In

39. A. bumpers

40. *Changing Rooms*

41. B. Brother

42. True. It's often piled in kitchens, hallways, extra bedrooms, and bathrooms.

43. True. The cast and crew see The Reveal unfold on a small monitor, often from a bathroom or a closet.

44. D. purple

45. False. Although there is a makeup artist on staff, everyone in the cast is responsible for dressing himself or herself.

46. pillow

47. Day Zero

48. True. This is done in an effort to maintain secrecy of both Reveals.

49. blue, green, orange, and red

50. B. one of the homeowners' garages

Section I: Photo Identification Answer

Page 9: Doug

?

Section 2:
the
people

Designers
Carpenters
Hosts

Everyone watches *Trading Spaces* for a different reason—the great design ideas, the projects that don't quite work out, homeowner reactions—but through it all, it's the cast members that make the show such a hit.

ople

1. Which *Trading Spaces* cast member appeared in commercials as a child?

   a. Amy Wynn
   b. Laurie
   c. Paige
   d. Gen

2. True or False? Frank was an aerobics instructor in his younger days.

3. Which film is not among Kia's prop work credits?

   a. *Men in Black*
   b. *12 Monkeys*
   c. *Independence Day*
   d. *Beloved*

4. The *Trading Spaces* designer who has never gone over budget is:

   a. Gen
   b. Kia
   c. Vern
   d. Edward

5. Vern's favorite soft drink is _____.

6. What shellfish do Doug and Ty try to put down Gen's hip waders while filming B-roll footage in Maine: George Road?

   a. lobster
   b. shrimp
   c. oyster
   d. crab

7. The only guest carpenter in the history of *Trading Spaces* is _____.

8. In Providence: Wallis Avenue, Frank uses his budget sparingly in order to buy the homeowners a _____.

9. In Las Vegas: Carlsbad Caverns, Doug "marries" _____ in a drive-through wedding chapel.

Answers begin on page 28

10. In Athens: County Road, Frank claims that he lost his hair in:
- **a.** a wood glue accident
- **b.** a painting accident
- **c.** a spackling accident
- **d.** a staining accident

11. True or False? Vern earned a degree from the University of Virginia in political science and biology.

12. True or False? Laurie is the first *Trading Spaces* cast member to remove an existing ceiling fan.

13. True or False? Vern's family built an addition onto its home using plans he drew as a senior in high school.

14. True or False? Frank displays mixed-media collages about fairy tales under the pseudonym of an old woman from Texas.

15. _____'s pants fall down while filming B-roll in Nazareth: First Street.

16. True or False? Hildi lives primarily in a Paris apartment near the Arc de Triomphe.

17. True or False? Doug still holds his junior high school's shot put record.

18. In her own home, Laurie claims to have four:
- **a.** canopy beds
- **b.** ceiling fans
- **c.** chaise lounges
- **d.** cuckoo clocks

19. In San Antonio: Ghostbridge, Hildi refers to herself as the _____.

20. Which *Trading Spaces* cast member has appeared in the fewest number of episodes?
- **a.** Laurie
- **b.** Vern
- **c.** Alex
- **d.** Doug

> Kia has never appeared on an episode with Gen or Laurie.

21. When Gen wears her hair in several little buns all over her head in Oakland: Webster Street, one of her homeowners uses them as a _____.

22. True or False? Gen's been commissioned by five clients to build a moss wall in their homes similar to the one she built in San Diego: Elm Ridge.

23. Which *Trading Spaces* cast member has appeared in ads for Enterprise Rent-A-Car?
   a. Alex
   b. Ty
   c. Paige
   d. Amy Wynn

24. True or False? In Austin: Aire Libre Drive, Ty recruits neighborhood kids to help construct a side table.

25. What do the two female homeowners present to Paige during the Key Swap in Plano: Shady Valley Road?
   a. a commemorative key chain
   b. a personalized paintbrush
   c. a teddy bear
   d. a decorative lamp

26. Which *Trading Spaces* cast member hasn't been caught turning a cartwheel by the camera?
   a. Laurie
   b. Doug
   c. Frank
   d. Paige

> Hildi leads the pack with *Trading Spaces* firsts: She removed the first ceiling fan, painted the first wood floor, ripped out the first carpet, and decorated the first bathroom.

Answers begin on page 28

27. Edward worked behind the scenes as the _____ for the first two seasons of *Trading Spaces*.

28. When people began buying Frank's paintings in galleries because of his *Trading Spaces* fame, he held a gallery exhibition of 25 canvases painted only with:

a. his portrait
b. a rooster
c. his handprint
d. his signature

29. True or False? The *Trading Spaces* crew hangs a sign outside each of Doug's rooms that reads Demolition in Progress.

30. Which film star provided the interior paint for Kia's home as a gift for making him tea each day on the set of a motion picture?

a. Bruce Willis
b. Brad Pitt
c. Mel Gibson
d. Samuel L. Jackson

01:39:30.25.2

Who designed this room?

31. Paige shows off her break-dancing skills in Texas: Sherwood Street by doing a _____ on Frank's rug.

32. In Santa Clara: Lafayette Street, _____ reminisces about her sorority days and talks about having to dress up like Carmen Miranda and sing "Kappa, Kappa-cabana" to the tune of Barry Manilow's "Copacabana."

33. Hildi's parents emigrated to the United States from _____.

34. Doug was inspired to pursue a career in theater after seeing a production of:
   a. *State Fair*
   b. *Oklahoma!*
   c. *The Sound of Music*
   d. *Flower Drum Song*

35. True or False? Laurie's son, who was born during *Trading Spaces'* third season, is named Garrison.

36. Hildi's beloved dog is named:
   a. Pluto
   b. Goofy
   c. Mickey
   d. Donald

Amy Wynn has appeared in more episodes than any other carpenter.

---

37. True or False? Gen worked as a graphic designer at MTV.

38. In Austin: Birdhouse Drive, Laurie's homeowners entice her to take a break by offering her:
   a. their undying devotion
   b. money
   c. a back rub
   d. Mexican food

39. True or False? In San Diego: Duenda Road, Frank kisses a dolphin at Sea World.

40. Amy Wynn's friends call her _____.

41. In high school, Vern was voted:
  a. Most Artistic
  b. Most Athletic
  c. Most Academic
  d. Most Acrobatic

Frank and Hildi are tied as the designer to appear in the most episodes. They've been in 47 episodes each.

42. True or False? Doug is the fourth of five brothers.

43. True or False? The cast combination of Doug, Vern, and Ty is the most common *Trading Spaces* design team.

44. Ty tells Alex in Orlando: Winterhaven that he thinks Doug's full name is Douglas _____ Wilson.

45. True or False? Both Paige and Laurie attended the same university.

Who designed this room?

46. Season I designer Dez Ryan created a custom _____ for each of her rooms.

47. True or False? Vern admits to having "the" Farrah Fawcet poster in his room as a kid in New Orleans: D'evereaux Street.

Doug, Hildi, and Edward all celebrate their birthdays on the fourth—but of different months. (November, April, and January, respectively)

48. Which *Trading Spaces* cast member is a self-proclaimed insomniac?
   a. Vern
   b. Gen
   c. Hildi
   d. Edward

49. True or False? In Long Island: Steuben Boulevard, Frank admits to a fear of heights.

Who designed this room?

50. Doug funded his move to New York City by throwing himself a benefit concert he called _____.

51. Which job did Doug not take on to make ends meet after moving to New York?
  a. handyman
  b. window washer
  c. carpet installer
  d. carpenter

52. True or False? While auditioning for *Trading Spaces*, Paige did a scene with Amy Wynn, who was building a mantel.

53. Doug designed a room for which cohost of *The View*?
  a. Barbara Walters
  b. Joy Behar
  c. Star Jones
  d. Meredith Viera

54. True or False? Amy Wynn's middle name is in honor of her great-aunt, who was named Wendy.

55. _____ was featured on an episode of TLC's *A Wedding Story*.

56. Which designer appeared in only one episode of *Trading Spaces*?
  a. Ronald
  b. Roderick
  c. Roberto
  d. Ricardo

Doug and Edward have worked together in only one episode: South Carolina: Sherborne Drive.

57. Kia considers _____ her business idol.

58. Paige's full name is _____.

59. True or False? Vern installed the first ceiling fan in *Trading Spaces* history.

60. What language do Hildi and her husband, Etienne, speak to one another?
   a. French
   b. Italian
   c. English
   d. Spanish

61. _____ has been over budget more than any other *Trading Spaces* designer.

Paige and Gen share a Prince connection, having worked at one of his clubs: Paige as a dancer and Gen as a waitress.

62. True or False? Hildi appears in a *Trading Spaces* episode wearing a grass skirt and a coconut bra.

63. Vern was inspired to become an architect by experiencing the work of _____.

64. While refinishing a dresser in Mississippi: Winsmere Way, Hildi throws handfuls of which article of clothing into the air:
   a. T-shirts
   b. pajama pants
   c. socks
   d. underwear

65. In Colorado: Berry Avenue, Gen sketches her table design, complete with measurements, on Amy Wynn's:
   a. arm
   b. forehead
   c. palm
   d. leg

66. Season I host Alex went on to host which reality dating show:
   a. *For Love or Money*
   b. *Joe Millionaire*
   c. *Mr. Personality*
   d. *The Bachelorette*

67. In Austin: Birdhouse Drive, _____ plays the saw.

68. In Pennsylvania: Victoria Drive, Doug sticks his _____ in a plate of brownies and tries to feed them to his homeowners.

69. Frank and his wife, Judy, operate their own _____ business named Mosey 'n Me.

70. What article of personalized clothing has Paige not worn on the show?
  a. UC Berkeley sweatpants
  b. a bowling shirt
  c. a soccer jersey
  d. a U.S. Airforce flight suit

71. Berkeley: Prospect Street, in which Doug and Gen redecorate a fraternity and sorority chapter room (respectively), is the first episode in which both designers _____.

72. The life-size nutcracker in Laurie's room in New Jersey: Tall Pines Drive is named _____.

73. True or False? For many years, Edward designed fabric slipcovers.

74. True or False? Paige has appeared in more *Trading Spaces* episodes than any other cast member.

Hildi is the only cast member to have appeared in episodes with every *Trading Spaces* cast member, including Dez, Roderick, and Handy Andy. The only exception? She hasn't worked with Carter.

---

75. True or False? Frank often wears a ring with the Green Lantern symbol on it.

76. _____ has worked as a stockbroker and a political campaign manager.

77. True or False? Season 1 designer Dez wore a different hat in each of her Designer Chats.

78. True or False? The *Trading Spaces* design team of Gen, Hildi, and Amy Wynn has worked together more than any other group of cast members.

79. Paige met her husband while they were both performing in the National Tour of:
a. *Cats*
b. *Beauty and the Beast*
c. *Saturday Night Fever*
d. *Chicago*

80. Ty does a running gag of using _____ as lotion, rubbing it into his hands, face, and neck in Philadelphia: Gettysburg Lane.

81. True or False? Amy Wynn is a vampire aficionado.

82. In Austin: Wampton Way, Gen wears her male homeowner's _____ on her head.

83. After completing a Cuban-inspired room in Los Angeles: Willoughby Avenue, Gen lights a celebratory cigar with a _____.

Who designed this room?

84. True or False? When preparing to redecorate a fraternity chapter room in Berkeley: Prospect Street, Doug throws everything in the room out the upstairs window.

Kia turned down a job propping Jennifer Lopez's movie *Jersey Girl* in order to take the job as a *Trading Spaces* designer. The dress that Amy Wynn wore in TLC's *A Makeover Story* was originally designed for Jennifer Lopez, who chose not to wear it for an event.

85. In Arlington: First Road, Doug drinks from a mug that reads:
   a. Kiss the Designer
   b. Damn, I'm Good
   c. Pat Me on the Back
   d. Check Me Out

86. True or False? In Los Angeles: Murietta Avenue, fans can see Laurie getting a (fake) *Trading Spaces* tattoo.

87. True or False? Paige has compared body piercings with Mel Gibson.

88. As a child, Vern's favorite comic series was:
   a. *Batman*
   b. *Archie*
   c. *Spiderman*
   d. *X-Men*

89. True or False? In France, Hildi is known as Madame Etienne Fougeron.

Gen and Hildi have worked together on seven episodes with Amy Wynn but have worked on only one with Ty.

Section 2: Answers

1. **A.** Amy Wynn

2. **True.** It's how he met his wife; she attended one of his classes.

3. **C.** *Independence Day*

4. **D.** Edward

5. **Diet Coke**

6. **A.** lobster

7. **Handy Andy of** *Changing Rooms*

8. **dishwasher**

9. **Hildi**

10. **C.** a spackling accident

11. **False.** His degree is in economics and chemistry.

12. **False.** Hildi starts the trend in Athens: County Road.

13. **False.** He drew the plans as a seventh grader.

14. **False.** "She" focuses on Old Testament stories.

15. **Vern**

16. **False.** Her home is near the Les Invalides monument.

17. **False.** He is the reigning high jumper.

18. **B.** ceiling fans

19. **Slipcover Queen**

20. **B.** Vern

21. **pincushion**

22. **True.** All of the homeowners live in Manhattan.

23. **C.** Paige

24. **False.** He rounds up the kids to help wash the *Trading Spaces* trailer.

25. **D.** a decorative lamp

26. **A.** Laurie

27. **sewing coordinator**

28. **D.** his signature

29. **False.** The sign reads Danger: Doug's Room.

30. **A.** Bruce Willis

31. **back spin**

32. **Laurie**

33. **Cuba**

34. **B.** *Oklahoma!*

35. **False.** His name is Gibson.

36. **A.** Pluto

37. **True**

38. **D.** Mexican food

39. **True.** He wears a wet suit too.

40. **Wynn**

41. **A.** Most Artistic

42. **True**

43. **False.** The three have appeared in only one episode together.

44. **Issues**

45. **True.** They both attended Southern Methodist University, Paige for dance and Laurie for broadcast journalism.

46. **lamp**

47. **True**

48. **D.** Edward

49. **True.** He sends his homeowner up a ladder to paint the dining room's cathedral ceiling.

50. **The Road to New York**

51. **C.** carpet installer

52. **False.** When Paige auditioned a mantel was being constructed, but Ty was the carpenter.

53. **A.** Barbara Walters

54. **False.** Wynn is short for William, her great-grandfather's name.

55. **Paige**

56. **B.** Roderick

57. **Oprah**

58. **Mindy Paige Davis Page**

59. **True.** He adds a white fan to a living room in Portland: Rosemont Avenue.

60. **D.** Spanish

61. **Hildi**

62. **False.** In Knoxville: Stubbs Bluff, Frank dons the hula outfit.

63. **IM Pei**

64. **D.** underwear

65. **C.** palm

66. **B.** *Joe Millionaire*

67. **Amy Wynn**

68. **feet**

69. **cross-stitch pattern**

70. **A.** UC Berkeley sweatpants

71. **go over budget**

72. **Nutty**

73. **False.** He designed beaded mother-of-the-bride dresses.

74. **True.** Paige filmed 105 episodes during Seasons 2 and 3, although only 104 have aired (the missing episode will air in Season 4).

75. **False.** His ring is embossed with the Superman symbol.

76. **Hildi**

77. **True**

78. **False.** They're tied with Gen, Vern, and Ty at seven episodes each.

79. **B.** *Beauty and the Beast*

80. **wood glue**

81. **True**

82. **boxer shorts**

83. **blowtorch**

84. **True.** Everything, including the couch!

85. **B.** Damn, I'm Good

86. **True**

87. **False.** Kia and Mel talked about their body jewelry while working together on the film *Signs*.

88. **D.** *X-Men*

89. **True.** It's her married name.

Section 2: Photo Identification Answers

Page 19: Frank

Page 21: Doug

Page 22: Vern

Page 26: Hildi

Section 3:

the

des

When it's all said and done, it's the completed room design that brings tears of joy or sadness to anxious homeowners. You remember The Reveals, but what about the room themes and their designer-given names?

igns

Bedrooms Feng Shui
Living Rooms
Denim Deluxe ?

1. **In Missouri: Sunburst Drive, both Gen and Vern design bedrooms that include:**
   a. stenciled lampshades
   b. closet doors decoupaged with family photos
   c. custom leather accents
   d. handmade feather accents

2. **In Long Island: Split Rock Road, Gen paints a large kitchen green, blue, and yellow after seeing a necklace made of _____ that the female homeowner often wears.**

> In Ft. Lauderdale: 59th Street, Hildi gets an amazing deal on a set of four yellow vintage Eames chairs to use in her retro kitchen design. The collector's item chairs cost only $25 each.

3. **Hildi redoes a kitchen with retro furnishings and colors in Ft. Lauderdale: 59th Street based on the homeowners' collection of:**
   a. metal lunchboxes
   b. vintage tablecloths
   c. diner menus
   d. Fiestaware dishes

4. **The only thing Doug did not do when transforming a Portland: Everett Street family room into an Art Deco theater is:**
   a. add a small popcorn machine
   b. place the chairs on graduated platforms
   c. install aisle lights
   d. create movie-theme wall sconces

5. **Gen titles her southwestern design for a Santa Fe: Feliz basement living room:**
   a. Cactus Country
   b. Azteca Techno
   c. Adobe Mod
   d. Mad for Mesas

6. **In Key West: Elizabeth Street, Gen titles her room design Caribbean _____.**

Answers begin on page 42

7. Amy Wynn talks Gen out of demolishing an entire wall in a basement rec room in Philadelphia: Galahad Road because of:

a. a lack of equipment
b. time constraints
c. homeowner protests
d. structural concerns

8. Doug adds _____ to his blue and white sunroom design in Philadelphia: Valley Road so the homeowners can check on their children as they play outside.

9. Gen's Retro Fly design for a New Orleans: D'evereaux Street den is based on:

a. a vintage tablecloth that Gen makes into floor pillows
b. an existing teal chair
c. the homeowners' desk from the mid-1950s
d. funky album covers Gen found at a flea market

The *Trading Spaces* designers have looked to various artists for inspiration, including Hans Hofmann, Georgia O'Keeffe, Henri Matisse, Adolph Gottlieb, Vincent Van Gogh, Jean Cocteau, Roy Lichtenstein, and Jackson Pollock.

---

10. Laurie chooses the dark aqua blue paint for a living room in Portland: Rosemont Avenue based on:

a. the shirt she plans to wear for the episode
b. the bay where the episode is being filmed (the paint color shares its name)
c. the fabric chosen for the draperies and throw pillows
d. the color of the sky in Bombay, where she recently traveled

11. Hildi names her dark pink office in Pennsylvania: Cresheim Road:

a. Mom's Lipstick Palace
b. Raspberry Daiquiri
c. Sexy Sherbet Dream
d. Pink Passion Pit

12. True or False? Kia designs a red and silver dining room in New Jersey: Catania Court, choosing her design colors from a ring she bought in Afghanistan.

13. True or False? When Hildi's homeowners in Knoxville: Forest Glen refuse to assist in painting a thin black line around the edge of the wood floor, Hildi decides to lay a black rug instead.

14. Gen's cigar box bedroom in Philadelphia: 22nd Street is inspired by the nation of _____.

15. In Annapolis: Fox Hollow, Gen and Laurie choose nearly identical paint colors, but they're named:
   a. Amber Cream and Buttermilk Fawn
   b. Serendipity and Aegean Sea
   c. Butterscotch and Muted Pumpkin
   d. Blush and Bashful

16. True or False? In Austin: Birdhouse Drive, Laurie tells Alex that she suspended a large framed piece of fabric in the middle of her room to help with the acoustics.

17. True or False? In Maple Glen: Fiedler Road, Gen looks to lilies for inspiration when choosing colors for a brown, cream, and red living room.

18. In Knoxville: Forest Glen, Doug titles his design for a bedroom Country:
   a. Urbane
   b. Comforts
   c. Unlimited
   d. Cozy

> Doug has named 28 of his 45 rooms.

19. When one of Hildi's homeowners won't let her dye the carpet orange in a Plano: Shady Valley Road bedroom, Hildi decides to:
   a. dye it anyway
   b. sprinkle orange flower petals across the carpet
   c. buy a large orange rug
   d. settle for the existing tan carpet

20. In Chicago: Edward Road, _____ designs a brown and yellow living room with an X motif on the furniture.

21. In Virginia: Gentle Heights Courts, Hildi redesigns a boy's bedroom by painting the walls blue, hanging a moon-shape light fixture, and suspending a mobile of the solar system to create a:

a. science fiction theme
b. mad scientist theme
c. space station theme
d. camping theme

22. Hildi's multicolor wall treatment for a girl's room in London: Garden Flat is a nod to the artist:

a. Roy Lichtenstein
b. Frida Kahlo
c. Ringo Starr
d. Jackson Pollock

23. Gen's teal and brown room design in New Orleans: D'evereaux Street titled Retro Fly is for a:

a. girl's bedroom
b. sunporch
c. kitchen
d. den

Who designed this room?

24. Gen tries to convince one of her homeowners in San Diego: Camino Mojado that Vern wants to explore new design avenues in their home, including:

a. the back alley
b. the workbench
c. the barnyard
d. the janitorial closet

25. True or False? The colors in Laurie's green and yellow living room in South Carolina: Innisbrook Lane are inspired by a Picasso print.

26. In Arlington: First Road, Hildi designs a bedroom with blue walls embellished with white airbrushed lines and silver accents to resemble a _____ box.

27. _____ has titled a room Bombay Meets Etouffee.

28. In Oregon: Alyssum Avenue, Gen uses graphic vintage napkins as inspiration. She later uses them to create _____ to accent the room.

Frank claims in Ft. Lauderdale: 59th Street to always make one of the legs different than the other three on any table he constructs.

29. True or False? Hildi designs a living room with stripes on the floor, the pillows, the walls, and the draperies in Colorado: Andes Way.

30. True or False? In Vegas: Carlsbad Caverns, Hildi gets inspiration from a brightly colored architectural rendering she purchased in India.

31. True or False? Gen designs a basement rec room based on a Sorry! gameboard in Philadelphia: Jeannes Street.

32. True or False? Vern redoes a bedroom for two young boys with a baseball theme in New Orleans: D'evereaux Street.

33. Doug has never titled a kitchen design:

a. Contempo-rribean Kitchen
b. Cocteau Country
c. Kitchen with a Dash of Kitsch
d. Tuscan Today

34. In San Diego: Wilbur Street, Frank creates a design that he refers to as a _____ meets tropical look.

35. In a Northampton: James Avenue living room, Frank paints the walls sage green, wraps rope around the coffee table legs, and builds a dinghy-inspired dog bed as part of a:
- **a.** Nantucket theme
- **b.** Grecian Isle theme
- **c.** Hilton Head resort theme
- **d.** Polynesian fishing village theme

36. True or False? Doug redecorates a living room in San Diego: Hermes Avenue with colors based on the homeowners' framed batik prints.

37. In Colorado: Berry Avenue, Gen chooses the colors for a kitchen based on:
- **a.** a pomegranate
- **b.** a strawberry
- **c.** an avocado
- **d.** an artichoke

Who designed this room?

38. Gen bases her colors in a living room in Washington, D.C.: Quebec Place on her favorite Thai soup made with:

a. coconut milk broth
b. goat milk broth
c. sheep milk broth
d. cow milk broth

39. True or False? Gen chooses colors for a kitchen based on the homeowners' green glass bottle collection in Oakland: Webster Street.

40. True or False? Laurie removes the piano from a living room in Portland: Rosemont Avenue because she doesn't think its wood tone complements her design.

41. Edward's homeowners in South Carolina: Sherborne Drive present him with an unusual fish-shape water pitcher they want to have displayed in the room. During The Reveal it can be seen on:

a. the dining table
b. a decorative shelf
c. the mantel
d. a side table

Who designed this room?

42. In Vegas: Woodmore Court, Gen tells Paige that the colors in her room design are inspired by a table setting at a restaurant that features bowls filled with:

    a. lemons and limes
    b. apples and oranges
    c. peaches and nectarines
    d. plums and grapes

43. In Maryland: Fairway Court, Doug designs a Pullman-theme room in a:

    a. living room
    b. bedroom
    c. dining room
    d. kitchen

44. True or False? Kia's exotic red and gold bedroom design in Indiana: Halleck Way is an homage to ancient Egypt.

45. Laurie paints a wall-size mural in a basement rec room in New Jersey: Tall Pines Drive in the style of the artist _____.

46. Because of the large wall he placed in the middle of the room in Scottsdale: Windrose Avenue, Doug names the bedroom Barrier but jokes that he should name it _____ because the homeowners' kids will chase each other in circles around it.

47. Vern uses the principles of feng shui in a living room in Providence: Phillips Street, adding bamboo plants for:

    a. personal growth
    b. mindfulness
    c. health
    d. wealth

48. In Austin: Aire Libre Drive, Kia sends her team throughout the house to pick items that will look good in the newly designed room. She calls the process Redecorating by _____,

49. Doug creates a graphic rectangular stencil for his red and white living room in Los Angeles: Willoughby Avenue based on the pattern on an existing _____.

50. Gen creates an _____ -theme tearoom on a sunporch in New York: Shore Road.

51. True or False? When Kia's homeowners nix her plans to hang vertical blinds in a basement TV room in New York: Half Hollow Turn, she returns the morning of Day 2 with fabric to make curtains instead.

52. In Plano: Bent Horn Court, Gen designs a multicolor playroom with a:
a. spiral motif
b. rainbow motif
c. polka-dot motif
d. balloon motif

53. In San Diego: Dusty Trail, Gen transforms a kitchen into a French:
a. *boucherie* (butcher shop)
b. *epicerie* (grocery)
c. *boulangerie* (bakery)
d. *fromagerie* (cheese shop)

54. True or False? Frank's lips headboard in an orange bedroom in Missouri: Sweetbriar Lane is modeled after his wife's lips.

55. In an Albuquerque: Gloria living room, Doug plays up his Wind in Our Sails title by:
a. setting up several fans around the room
b. stenciling sailboats at the ceiling line
c. hanging wind chimes on each side of the entertainment center
d. suspending a large white canvas from the ceiling

56. In San Diego: Hermes Avenue, Laurie disguises a window with a large wooden frame covered in bamboo place mats in order to:
a. save money on buying more fabric
b. visually center the window on the wall
c. give Amy Wynn something to do
d. hide an unsightly view

57. In Boston: Ashfield Street, Gen designs a dark blue bedroom for a young girl with motifs and colors inspired by the country of _____.

58. True or False? In New York: Linda Court, Doug titles his living room design Mediterranean Trust Me.

59. In Missouri: Sunburst Drive, Gen creates a brown and cream bedroom design inspired by Argentine cowboys, also known as _____.

 Answers begin on page 42

60. When the grout on Hildi's flooring tiles dries white instead of dark gray in San Diego: Elm Ridge, she runs to the store to buy _____ to conceal the problem.

61. In Quakerstown: Quakers Way, Hildi calls the blue and white basement family room painted with several perpendicular lines:
a. Pythagorean design
b. orthogonal design
c. precipitous design
d. dodecahedronic design

62. In Pennsylvania: Bryant Court, _____ names her pink and green girls' room Zany for Zinnias.

63. Gen paints a living room in Los Angeles: Irving Street cream, green, and pink based on:
a. lilies
b. orchids
c. roses
d. hydrangeas

Who designed this room?

Section 3: Answers

1. **C.** custom leather accents

2. **sea glass**

3. **D.** Fiestaware dishes

4. **A.** add a small popcorn machine

5. **C.** Adobe Mod

6. **Chill**

7. **D.** structural concerns

8. **binoculars**

9. **B.** an existing teal chair

10. **B.** the bay where the episode is being filmed (the paint color shares its name)

11. **A.** Mom's Lipstick Palace

12. **False.** Gen designed the room and wears the ring in several episodes.

13. **False.** She and Alex paint the floor despite the homeowners' protests.

14. **Cuba**

15. **C.** Butterscotch and Muted Pumpkin

16. **False.** It divides the sitting area and the dining area.

17. **True**

18. **A.** Urbane

19. **B.** sprinkle orange flower petals across the carpet

20. **Laurie**

21. **D.** camping theme

22. **D.** Jackson Pollock

23. **D.** den

24. **C.** the barnyard

25. **False.** It is a Van Gogh print of a butterfly.

26. **Tiffany**

27. **Gen**

28. **pillows**

29. **False.** The striped room designed for that episode is Vern's creation.

30. **False.** She purchased the print in London.

31. **False.** She uses a Scrabble board and even frames one to hang on the wall.

32. **False.** He chooses a soccer theme.

33. **C.** Kitchen with a Dash of Kitsch

34. **British Colonial**

35. **A.** Nantucket theme

36. **False.** Gen chooses the room's colors based on the prints.

37. **D.** an artichoke

38. **A.** coconut milk broth

39. **False.** The homeowners collect bottles made of blue glass.

40. **False.** Ty doesn't believe the floor joists are strong enough to support the piano in the area of the room in which Laurie wants to place it.

41. **C.** the mantel

42. **D.** plums and grapes

43. **B.** bedroom

44. **True.** She even attempts to build a pyramid fountain.

45. **Henri Matisse**

46. **Racetrack**

47. **C.** health

48. **Relocating**

49. **pillow**

50. **Asian**

51. **True.** The homeowners are very relieved!

52. **C.** polka-dot motif

53. **A.** *boucherie* (butcher shop)

54. **False.** He tells Paige during the Designer Chat that he used her lips for inspiration.

55. **D.** suspending a large white canvas from the ceiling

56. **B.** visually center the window on the wall

57. **Morocco**

58. **False.** Frank gives his yellow living room, which he designed for that episode, the name.

59. **gauchos**

60. **two black rugs**

61. **B.** orthogonal design

62. **Laurie**

63. **B.** orchids

Section 3: Photo Identification Answers

Page 35: Gen

Page 37: Vern

Page 38: Edward

Page 41: Laurie

Section 4:
the
pro

?

?

MDF, a hot glue gun, paint, found objects, metal flashing, and rain gutters. Put them all together and you have the ingredients that truly bring a room to life the *Trading Spaces* way.

jects

ceiling fans   lamps
pyramid fountain
paintings

?

1. In New York: Sherwood Drive, Vern and his homeowners paint a phrase on the wall that reads:

 a. "Good friends are a gift from above"
 b. "Where your treasure is, there will be your heart"
 c. "A single candle can brighten the darkness"
 d. "Dream it to do it"

2. When the furniture Hildi spray-painted magenta is rained on and is ruined in Seattle: 56th Place she solves the problem by:

 a. scattering floor pillows for seating
 b. using them anyway
 c. buying new sofas
 d. sewing impromptu slipcovers

> Hildi has painted upholstered furniture using a paint sprayer three times over the course of the series in Albuquerque: Gloria, Seattle: 56th Place, and San Antonio: Ghostbridge.

3. In a Seattle: 137th Street living room, Frank creates a no-sew valance with:

 a. sheet metal and small carriage bolts
 b. place mats and clothespins
 c. shower curtains and cup hooks
 d. burlap and ribbons

4. Frank uses 4x4s and license plates in a California: Abbeywood Lane living room to make:

 a. bookends
 b. decorative art
 c. wall shelves
 d. candleholders

5. In California: Corte Rosa, Laurie suspends a board and uses it to drape pieces of fabric over the four corners of the bed, making a:

 a. Danish filigree canopy
 b. Spanish concha canopy
 c. Grecian lattice canopy
 d. French tester canopy

6. In her blue glass kitchen in Oakland: Webster Street, Gen personalizes _____ with family art and pictures.

Answers begin on page 72

7. Hildi's female homeowner doesn't have a putty knife to texture the living room walls for homework in Florida: Night Owl Lane, so she uses a _____ instead.

8. In New Jersey: Lafayette Street, Vern makes an architectural drawing of the exterior of the house to hang in the room on:
a. blueprint paper
b. vellum
c. fabric
d. poster board

9. In an Oakland: Webster Street living room, Hildi wires _____ on a copper mesh fireplace surround.

10. In a New York: Sherwood Drive bedroom, Doug constructs a water fountain that stands _____ feet tall.

11. In Key West: Elizabeth Street, Gen decoupages a wall with pages from a _____ -year-old book.

12. In a North Carolina: Southerby Drive bedroom, Doug paints wall-size _____ murals.

13. In a Delta Gamma chapter room in Santa Clara: Lafayette Street, Laurie stencils yellow _____ on the walls.

14. In his Zen Buddhist Asian dining room in Cincinnati: Sturbridge Road, Doug creates _____ with metal flashing.

Vern, Frank, and Kia are the only *Trading Spaces* designers to install ceiling fans in their rooms.

15. The custom kitchen table that Hildi designs in Ft. Lauderdale: 59th St. is made of:
a. antique oak
b. wrought iron
c. acrylic
d. chrome and glass

16. In a New York: Sherwood Drive bedroom, Vern creates a 4-foot-tall wall clock using _____ as the numbers.

17. In a music-theme kitchen in Pennsylvania: Cresheim Road, Kia fashions a _____ into a pot rack.

18. Kia names her paint colors for an Indianapolis: Halleck Way bedroom Tut Wine and _____ Gold.

19. In a San Diego: Fairfield office, Kia hangs soccer cleats on the bulletin board to hold:
a. pencils
b. phone messages
c. paper clips
d. sticky notes

20. In an Oregon: Alyssum Avenue bedroom, Hildi uses fabric paint to monogram plain white bed linens with the letter _____.

21. In Miami: Miami Place, Hildi designs a circular entertainment center to be constructed in quarters and placed in the center of the living room, but Ty only has time to make _____ sections.

22. In Florida: Night Owl Lane, Edward designs a headboard with decoratively framed:
a. mirrors
b. bulletin boards
c. family photos
d. fabric scraps

23. In a black and yellow dining room in Pennsylvania: Bryant Court, Hildi fills flower vases with _____.

24. The only thing Doug keeps from the original fraternity chapter room in his final design in Berkeley: Prospect Street is:
a. a mounted deer head
b. a pair of beer-theme lights
c. a composite of the fraternity members
d. a large poster of a swimsuit model

25. In a New York: Whitlock Road bedroom, Amy Wynn doesn't consult Doug before tweaking his design for:

a. a headboard

b. side tables

c. wall shelves

d. an armoire

26. In a Maine: Joseph Drive bedroom, Frank attaches a large clear plastic envelope to the wall. The envelope holds a pencil drawing of _____.

27. In a pink New Jersey: Lafayette Street living room, Frank adds a tall shelf to display the homeowners' collection of _____.

28. True or False? In San Diego: Elm Ridge, Hildi removes the existing carpet in order to lay exposed subflooring tiles in a bachelor's bedroom.

29. True or False? When Doug doesn't have the money in his budget for coffee table legs in Washington, D.C.: Cleveland Park, he improvises by filling plastic tumblers with plaster of Paris.

Who designed this room?

30. In a Scott Airforce Base: Ash Creek living/dining room, Kia uses gray parachutes as:

a. window treatments
b. slipcovers
c. place mats
d. framed wall art

31. In a living room in Washington, D.C.: Cleveland Park, Dez designs a custom three-headed Medusa lamp with spiky light bulbs and wraps _____ around the base and heads.

32. In Orlando: Winter Song Drive, Doug's female homeowner and Paige take the tiles off the existing bar using:

a. hammers
b. pliers
c. crowbars
d. rubber mallets

33. In New York: Half Hollow Turn, Paige applies spray paint too heavily to the concrete stepping-stones that will serve as the base of Frank's coffee table and runs out of paint. In order to purchase more:

a. Paige asks Amy Wynn to return some wood
b. Paige and Frank host an impromptu bake sale
c. Paige asks Kia to give Frank any excess funds from her budget
d. Paige takes up a collection among the cast and crew

34. In a Colorado: Berry Avenue kitchen, Gen indicates where each family member should sit by personalizing chair slipcovers with:

a. black-and-white photos of each person's head
b. their zodiac signs
c. their initials
d. a picture of their favorite foods

35. True or False? Gen has covered kitchen light fixtures with metal colanders five times during the course of the series.

36. True or False? With no money left in his budget to furnish an eating area in a Pennsylvania: Gorski Lane bedroom, Doug sends Ty to scavenge through the trash for enough wood scraps to build a breakfast table and two chairs.

37. True or False? For his jungle-influenced bedroom in Pennsylvania: Gorski Lane, Doug paints a large-scale giraffe print on all four walls.

38. When the TV cabinet Kia designs falls over in Miami: Ten Court, breaking the mirrors she framed to make doors, she hangs one of the now-empty frames on the wall, writing a note to the homeowners that reads:
  a. "Oops!"
  b. "*Trading Spaces* rules"
  c. "Too bad, so sad"
  d. "We are sorry"

39. The metal sculpture that Edward fabricates for a Missouri: Sweetbriar Lane bedroom is created from:
  a. a window well liner
  b. strips of roof flashing
  c. a furnace cover
  d. a car bumper

40. In Virginia: Gentle Heights Court, Kia uses heavy chain to suspend the:
  a. armoire
  b. bedside tables
  c. television
  d. bed

41. Frank builds a headboard in a Colorado: Stoneflower Drive bedroom that mimics a:
  a. string bass
  b. desert horizon
  c. skyline
  d. clam shell

42. True or False? In an Indiana: River Valley Drive living room, Doug hangs a large image of his foot painted on one long custom-built canvas.

43. Frank builds a coffee table by using an existing _____ as the tabletop in a New Jersey: Perth Road living room.

44. True or False? Gen enlarges a suggestive photo of the female homeowner and hangs it above the fireplace in a Houston: Sawdust Street living room.

45. The mixture for Laurie's faux tortoise shell finish that's used on a coffee table in Miami: 168/83rd Street does not include:

a. powdered pigment
b. malt vinegar
c. dishwashing liquid
d. egg whites

46. Hildi photocopies images of _____ to create wall art for a purple and gray California: Peralta Street quadrant living room.

47. True or False? Hildi spends $700—70 percent of her budget—on the lumber used only for the bed and a bench in a Chicago: Spaulding Avenue bedroom.

48. In Providence: Phillips Street, Hildi groups several silver _____ on the wall of a living room to create a decorative statement.

49. Frank builds a _____ -inspired dog bed in a Northampton: James Avenue living room.

Who designed this room?

50. In a young boy's bedroom in Orlando: Winterhaven, Doug builds a headboard using limbs from a _____ tree.

51. True or False? In Vegas: Carlsbad Caverns, Hildi uses four alleged stripper poles to create a four-poster look around the existing bed.

52. When Hildi's homeowners in Austin: Wyoming Valley Drive point out that their neighbors don't drink or keep alcohol in their home, Hildi changes her plans for a wine rack and makes a _____ instead.

53. Kia adds an exotic touch to a bedroom in Virginia: Gentle Heights Court by installing two wooden columns purchased in _____.

54. True or False? In Chicago: Fairview Avenue, Gen uses sweaters to upholster two small side chairs.

55. On a Colorado: Cherry Street living room wall, Gen hangs several antlers from:
   a. gazelles
   b. moose
   c. jackelopes
   d. deer

56. Laurie constructs an art piece for her neoclassical room design in Philadelphia: Valley Road by wrapping her male homeowner's _____ in papier mâché.

57. True or False? In Los Angeles: Elm Street, Gen uses an oxidizing paint technique for the second time in the series on two filing cabinets that support the new corner desk.

58. Gen attempts to dye white fabric orange to use as slipcovers in Chicago: Fairview Avenue, but they turn out _____ instead.

59. Paige realizes in Miramar: Avenue 164 that Doug did not purchase the dirt she's using to plant flowers for the room when she sees _____ in it.

60. In a Los Angeles: Springdale Drive dining room, Vern designs a multiarm halogen chandelier with gold vellum shades printed with a _____ motif.

61. In a boy's bedroom in Long Island: Dover Court, Vern suspends various items from the ceiling, including:

   a. soccer balls and cleats

   b. hockey pennants and a hockey stick

   c. a working train track and toy airplanes

   d. camping lanterns and glow-in-the-dark stars

62. Vern adds a live touch to a serene bedroom in New York: Sherwood Drive by installing wall vases filled with:

   a. beta fish

   b. hermit crabs

   c. air ferns

   d. Sea Monkeys

63. In San Diego: Dusty Trail, Gen and her team make humanlike figures out of raw meat, take pictures of them, and display the photos in the finished room, calling them:

   a. butcher boys

   b. meat puppets

   c. meal men

   d. beefcakes

> Laurie's removed the most ceiling fans, having taken down 14 of them.

64. Hildi uses sage chenille fabric in an Austin: La Costa Drive sewing room to reupholster a vintage:

   a. shampoo chair

   b. barber chair

   c. shoe shine chair

   d. dentist chair

65. Paige and Laurie's homeowners think that the black and white custom artwork Laurie paints for a living room in Santa Monica: Ocean Park looks like:

   a. soccer balls

   b. newspaper columns

   c. cow hides

   d. prison uniforms

66. True or False? In Colorado: Andes Way, Frank nails wooden stars to the living room ceiling.

67. In a Philadelphia: Jeannes Street living room, Vern and his homeowners run out of time during their holiday-influenced room makeover and must eliminate Vern's designs for:

a. radiator covers

b. bench seating

c. a tri-level mantel

d. storage for the homeowners' DVD collection

68. When Frank tells Ty to let his creativity flow when designing a desk for a girl's bedroom in Scottsdale: Bell Road, Ty constructs it to look like a:

a. monkey

b. cat

c. turtle

d. dinosaur

69. In Berkeley: Prospect Street, Doug constructs two large green and orange circular ottomans for a _____ fraternity chapter room.

70. In a Mexican-theme kitchen in Austin: Wing Road, Gen paints the linoleum floor:

a. blue

b. multicolor to look like a serape

c. orange

d. brown and gray to create a faux stone look

71. To avoid painting the homeowners' brick fireplace in Seattle: 137th Street, Doug builds a _____ to achieve the look he wants.

72. In Austin: Wing Road, Gen adds a metallic touch to her Mexican kitchen design by attaching a tall pasta pot to:

a. a barstool

b. the light fixture

c. the wall

d. a lazy Susan

73. Vern dyes the white fabric he later sews into slipcovers in Seattle: Dakota Street with _____.

74. In a basement family room in Chicago: Fairview Avenue, Gen installs a new wooden plank ceiling made of:

a. oak
b. pine
c. maple
d. cherry

75. Doug paints figures directly on the wall in a Maryland: Village Green bedroom that are in the style of the artist:

a. Alexander Calder
b. Pablo Picasso
c. Edgar Degas
d. Henri Matisse

76. True or False? In a London: Garden Flat bedroom, Gen frames several small pieces of Arabic newsprint.

77. Frank uses a saddle in a Texas: Sutton Court living room to make:

a. a footstool
b. a coffee table base
c. a child's rocking horse
d. decorative art

78. In a Plano: Shady Valley Road bedroom, Hildi installs 12-inch-tall orange _____.

79. In an Indiana: Fieldhurst Lane bedroom, Doug creates custom paintings of:

a. basketballs and basketball hoops
b. barns and haystacks
c. wheat and corn
d. race cars and checkered flags

80. In Colorado: Stoneflower Drive, Doug separates a living room and kitchen by:

a. hanging four canister light fixtures between the two spaces
b. stapling window sheers to the ceiling between the two spaces
c. building an armoire between the two spaces
d. installing a pleated metal screen between the two spaces

81. True or False? In a pink California: Peralta Street dining room, Doug upholsters white dining chairs with lime green T-shirts.

82. Gen covers an entire bedroom wall with 6x6 wood squares in Oregon: Alyssum Avenue and paints them various shades of gold, green, and black, except for one, which she paints _____.

83. True or False? Laurie transforms a captain's wheel into a candelabra in the Delta Gamma chapter room in Santa Clara: Lafayette Street.

84. In several rooms, Doug uses a _____ technique to coat the walls with tinted, waxed plaster.

85. In his Going Ballistic living room in Quakertown: Quakers Way, Doug constructs a new sofa and makes the feet from:
a. gazing balls
b. kickballs
c. bowling balls
d. soccer balls

86. True or False? In Berkeley: Prospect Street, Gen makes wall art for a sorority chapter room by having her team take black-and-white photos of herself and Paige.

Who designed this room?

87. In Boston: Institute Road, Frank's homeowners paint a Shakespeare quote on the family room wall that reads:

   a. "All things are ready if our minds be so"

   b. "To sleep, perchance, to dream"

   c. "We are such stuff as dreams are made on"

   d. "And be you blithe and bonny"

88. Doug attempts to make a decorative art piece for a Quakertown: Quakers Way living room by wrapping a kickball with _____.

89. When making faux potted cacti in Texas: Sutton Court, Frank does not use:

   a. cucumbers

   b. flower blossoms

   c. eggplants

   d. Brussels sprouts

90. True or False? Gen customizes a small white chandelier in a New Jersey: Catania Court dining room by wiring strands of beads to it.

91. In Oregon: Alsea Court, Frank upholsters the dining chairs for a Mexican kitchen with _____ fabric.

92. Gen makes a _____ out of an obi in Seattle: 56th Place.

93. To deal with a badly stained floor in a Los Angeles: Willoughby Avenue living room, Gen and her homeowners:

   a. apply bleach and detergent to the floor

   b. sew together several area rugs into a large carpet

   c. paint the floor black

   d. rent a floor sander and spend much of the two days refinishing the floor

94. True or False? In Philadelphia: Strathmore Road, Dez builds an end table lamp from a wheelbarrow.

95. For a Pennsylvania: Gorski Lane bedroom, Frank builds a custom wall art installation from:

   a. road construction signs

   b. barbecue grill components

   c. chain-link fence

   d. asphalt shingles

Answers begin on page 72

96. In an Oregon: Alsea Court kitchen, Frank paints a serape on the:

a. floor
b. ceiling
c. dining table
d. cabinets

97. In Austin: La Costa Drive, Hildi explains that the technique of horizontally attaching fabric to walls is called _____.

98. Instead of painting it, Gen darkens the grain of a newly built Danish modern entertainment center in Los Angeles: Willoughby Avenue using:

a. tea bags
b. a light stain
c. a blowtorch
d. tung oil

99. When Kia's plan to cover copper blinds with fabric hits a snag in a San Diego: Fairfield office/gameroom she:

a. hangs up the few completed blinds anyway
b. eliminates the project and leaves the windows bare
c. hangs simple window scarves instead
d. runs out to buy new blinds that put her over budget

100. Kia embellishes a _____ in Indianapolis: Halleck Way by hot-gluing plastic palm fronds to it.

101. In Philadelphia: Gettysburg Lane, Vern gets an unexpected head start on his design for a living room because:

a. the walls are already painted the color he planned to use
b. the homeowners removed the existing wallpaper before he arrived
c. the furniture had already been removed from the room
d. the homeowners had ripped out the existing stained carpet

102. Kia customizes an existing room screen in an Indianapolis: Halleck Way bedroom with the homeowners' names by painting hieroglyphics on it that read:

a. Kia loves David and Noel
b. David and Noel love *Trading Spaces*
c. Pharaoh David and Queen Noel
d. David loves Noel

103. Frank covers an entire wall in an Oregon: Alsea Court kitchen with metal flashing hung in a:

a. patchwork motif
b. series of vertical stripes
c. basketweave pattern
d. concentric rectangle design

104. In a Maryland: Village Green bedroom, Gen covers a small nook by decoupaging the walls with:

a. colored tissue paper
b. pages from a vintage fashion magazine
c. sewing patterns
d. black-and-white family photos

105. In Maryland: Fairway Court, Vern hangs 100 _____ from the bed canopy edge in a bedroom.

106. True or False? In a girl's bedroom in Boston: Ashfield Street, Gen creates shades for wall sconces with place mats that have a large image of a zinnia.

Who designed this room?

107. In Seattle: 56th Place, Hildi uses magenta and taupe fabric to "tent" a:

    a. basement rec room

    b. guest bedroom

    c. kids' playroom

    d. dining room

108. Hildi staples more than _____ silk floral blooms to the walls of a bathroom in Mississippi: Golden Pond.

109. True or False? In Maple Glen: Fiedler Road, Laurie pins photocopies of vintage botanical postcards to the wall of a living room.

110. Doug creates artwork for a bedroom in Boston: Institute Road by framing:

    a. autumn leaves

    b. palm fronds

    c. pressed flowers

    d. ivy vines

111. True or False? For a Long Island: Split Rock Road kitchen, Gen successfully drills through rocks to make tealight candleholders.

112. The swing Vern hangs from the ceiling in a boy's bedroom in Long Island: Dover Court is made from recycled tires and resembles a:

    a. motorcycle

    b. horse

    c. plane

    d. rowboat

113. True or False? In Long Island: Dover Court, Vern pays neighborhood kids $5 for prints of planes, trains, and automobiles to include in the room design.

114. In Lawrenceville: Pine Lane, Hildi designs an organic living room with a tree limb valance and an armoire covered in:

    a. sticks

    b. dried leaves

    c. craft moss

    d. berry garland

115. For a New York: Whitlock Road bedroom, _____ frames strips of wood veneer to create custom wall art.

116. True or False? In Plano: Bent Horn Court, Gen sends Alex on a mission to find objects around the house with different textures to frame and hang in a kids' playroom.

117. In a San Diego: Camino Mojado television room, Vern frames photocopies of Hollywood legends on vellum to make:
a. coasters
b. side table tops
c. candleholders
d. wall art

118. True or False? Over the course of the series, Vern has installed headboards using basketwoven fabric, upholstered leather squares, and bent tree branches.

Kia has installed the most ceiling fans. She's hung three of them.

119. In a New Jersey: Sam Street bedroom, Hildi builds seating out of small wooden platforms stacked with pillows that she names:
a. Toe Stubbers
b. Otto-Minis
c. Mule Stools
d. Pillow Pods

120. In California: Via Jardin, Vern's team refers to the existing red kitchen walls as _____ Red.

121. In his design for a Santa Fe: Feliz kitchen, Vern includes a planter of:
a. oat grass
b. wheat grass
c. Kentucky bluegrass
d. alfalfa grass

122. Gen covers a bedroom wall in San Diego: Elm Ridge with real moss from the state of _____.

123. True or False? In a Boston: Institute Road family room, Kia creates wooden cutouts painted to look like Elizabethan musicians for the wall.

124. In a Boston: Ashfield Street girl's room, Laurie fashions nontraditional closet doors from:

a. paper clips and acrylic squares
b. printed bed sheets
c. multicolor ribbons
d. wooden beads and yarn

125. True or False? Vern uses picture frames filled with postcards and drawings as window shutters in a bedroom in New York: Sherwood Drive.

126. In a Long Island: Steuben Boulevard bedroom, Edward paints the furniture tops and wall sconce boards with a faux finish that resembles:

a. lapis
b. tortoise shell
c. malachite
d. Italian marble

127. In a San Diego: Hermes Avenue kitchen, homeowners veto Laurie's plans to cover a large mirror frame with:

a. grosgrain ribbon
b. mosaic tiles
c. seashells
d. dried flowers

128. When Hildi uses tissue paper to make her own wallpaper in a Cincinnati: Melrose Avenue kitchen, she embellishes it with stenciled _____.

129. When Gen's homeowners aren't able to quickly create M. C. Escher-inspired drawings in a Washington, D.C.: Quebec Place living room, she decides to frame _____ as wall art instead.

130. In her Cuban-style bedroom for Philadelphia: 22nd Street, Gen makes picture frames out of _____.

131. Amy Wynn rebuilds Kia's cedar arbor for the garden bedroom in Pennsylvania: Victoria Drive because the original:

a. was built with the wrong lumber
b. isn't sturdy enough to support a person's weight
c. is too big to fit through the doorway
d. was built to the wrong dimensions

132. True or False? In Orlando: Lake Catherine, Hildi covers a bedroom ceiling with aluminum foil squares.

133. In a Missouri: Sweetbriar Lane bedroom, Edward dresses up a basic hanging light fixture by wrapping the piece entirely in:
  a. copper wire
  b. raffia
  c. twine
  d. pearls

134. In Houston: Sawdust Street, Doug builds a large L-shape couch and sews long bolster pillows using batting and:
  a. cardboard shipping tubes
  b. dowel rods
  c. pool noodles
  d. PVC pipe

135. In a Seattle: 56th Place living room, Gen uses cedar flowerpots as:
  a. CD storage
  b. wall shelving
  c. footstools
  d. picture frames

136. True or False? In an Orlando: Smith Street efficiency apartment, Hildi dyes the carpet brown.

137. In Maple Glen: Fiedler Road, Laurie embellishes a set of pillow shams by:
  a. sewing on bamboo place mats
  b. hot-gluing burgundy fringe around the edges
  c. stenciling monograms
  d. tie-dyeing them orange and gold

138. True or False? In California: Peralta Street, Hildi covers a brick fireplace with broken gray and purple tiles in her quadrant living room.

139. In a San Diego: Hermes Avenue living room, Gen dresses up baby bumpers installed for safety on a step by covering the plastic guards with:
  a. craft fur
  b. felt
  c. self-adhesive foam
  d. shag carpet

140. Gen uses an _____ as a stencil for the wall polka dots in a Plano: Bent Horn Court playroom.

141. Doug designs a wooden _____ using a rope and pulley system in a living room in New Jersey: Lincroft.

142. In an Orlando: Whisper Lake living room, Hildi transforms wicker chicken cages into:
    a. side tables
    b. trash cans
    c. light fixtures
    d. candleholders

143. True or False? Frank hangs a large hand-painted mermaid in a teal living room in Key West: Elizabeth Street.

144. In a Pennsylvania: Victoria Drive garden-theme bedroom, Kia creates a coverlet out of _____,

Who designed this room?

145. Hildi removes the drop ceiling tiles in a Providence: Phillips Street living room and replaces them with:
   a. faux stained-glass panels
   b. fabric woven through the metal supports
   c. stained wood
   d. sheets of metal flashing

146. Gen designs a special display area in a teenager's bedroom in Cincinnati: Sturbridge Road for a collection of:
   a. state coffee mugs
   b. keepsake snow globes
   c. hand-painted thimbles
   d. souvenir spoons

147. In Philadelphia: East Avenue, Hildi paints one wall of a living room with a large Roy Lichtenstein-inspired portrait of _____.

148. In Frank's karaoke-theme basement in Knoxville: Stubbs Bluff, he designs a round coffee table painted to look like a _____.

149. True or False? In Indianapolis: Halleck Way, Kia transforms a bedroom into ancient Egypt, complete with a pyramid-shape fountain.

150. To make an art piece for a San Diego: Elm Ridge bedroom, Hildi creates a bust by wrapping _____ in copper mesh.

151. True or False? In Miami: Ten Court, Kia builds a clam-shape head- and footboard.

152. In a Nazareth: First Street living room, Vern uses fabric with a taupe and blue wave motif to sew _____.

153. True or False? In Athens: County Road, Laurie hangs a wooden swing from the ceiling of a girl's lavender bedroom.

154. In a Philadelphia: Strathmore Road living room, Frank designs a child-size:
   a. fort
   b. tent
   c. teepee
   d. playhouse

155. In Ft. Lauderdale: 59th Street, Frank creates a tri-panel sunset-theme art piece for an orange living room using _____ instead of canvas because it's cheaper.

156. In a wine importer's kitchen in Orlando: Lake Catherine, Vern creates a chandelier using 36 _____ suspended in an aluminum frame.

157. True or False? For a bedroom in Maine: Joseph Drive, Doug and Paige make custom candleholders with metal pipe nipples and flanges.

158. Doug uses rough-hewn cuts of poplar in Pennsylvania: Victoria Drive on armoire doors and as wall art. The lumber is known as:
a. bark-edge
b. first-cut
c. fence-grade
d. log-strip

159. In a retro basement office in New Orleans: D'evereaux Street, Gen creates a room screen using:
a. aluminum screening
b. metal cable
c. chain link
d. metal flashing

160. In Knoxville: Stubbs Bluff, Doug creates a large art display for a kitchen by spray painting a shovel and pitchfork white. He originally planned to coat the pair in _____, but they weren't drying as quickly as desired.

161. The Chinese characters Edward paints on a piece of custom artwork in a Florida: Night Owl Lane bedroom mean:
a. night and day
b. man and woman
c. health and wealth
d. luck and love

162. In a New York: Whitlock Road bedroom, Gen uses yarn to embellish a white bedspread with:
a. orange asterisks
b. teal squares
c. violet Xs
d. pink French knots

163. In California: Peralta Street, Hildi attempts to drill through four large stones to create legs for a circular ottoman, but when it doesn't work she decides to use:
- **a.** adhesive
- **b.** metal brackets
- **c.** rope
- **d.** hook-and-loop tape

164. In San Diego: Duenda Road, Vern and his male homeowner joke that the wall vases Vern hangs in the living room can hold flowers or _____,

165. True or False? Over the course of the series, Doug has designed light fixtures from silver fruit bowls, candy dishes, and rain gutter components.

166. In a Miami: 168/83rd Street bedroom, Dez stencils the furniture with Xs after the homeowners talked her out of stenciling the pieces with _____.

167. True or False? In Quakertown: Quakers Way, Hildi makes art for a basement family room by filling acrylic box frames with different types of candy.

Who designed this room?

168. True or False? In Washington, D.C.: Cleveland Park, Frank adds seating to a basement rec room by creating a beanbag sofa.

169. In a Miami: 168/83rd Street bedroom, Dez customizes the lampshades by stenciling them with:
a. tea roses
b. dragons
c. hearts and ducks
d. Chinese characters

> The *Trading Spaces* carpenters often use MDF (medium density fiberboard), a strong, sturdy alternative to expensive plywood.

170. In a New Jersey: Lafayette Street living room, Vern enlarges pictures of the homeowners' baby and uses them as _____.

171. In his White Whoa living room in New Jersey: Manitoba Trail, the one new item the homeowners specifically ask Doug for is a:
a. doorbell
b. screen door
c. TV stand
d. ceiling fan

172. The number of the boy's race car bed Vern designs in Long Island: Dover Court is _____.

173. In a California: Abbeywood Lane living room, Hildi paints the walls black and covers them in 120 stripes of:
a. decorative molding
b. lightly stained 1x2
c. stenciled floral vines
d. embroidered fabric trim

174. In Orlando: Gotha Furlong, Gen uses a 1970s tablecloth to make:
a. a duvet cover
b. draperies
c. an upholstered bench
d. throw pillows

175. Dez creates custom lamps using the husband's _____ as bases in a living room in Lawrenceville: Pine Lane.

176. In a tan and lavender kitchen in Knoxville: Stubbs Bluff, Doug hangs silver kitchen utensils on the:
- **a.** cabinets
- **b.** walls
- **c.** backs of the dining chairs
- **d.** soffit

177. In a pink office in Pennsylvania: Cresheim Road, Hildi lays _____ squares as flooring.

178. Gen sews pillows from pinstriped suit jackets and uses _____ as curtain tiebacks in a bedroom in Texas: Sherwood Street.

179. In Austin: Birdhouse Drive, Frank paints his only *Trading Spaces* "chicken," which is actually a:
- **a.** hen
- **b.** chick
- **c.** rooster
- **d.** duck

180. True or False? In New Orleans: Jacob Street, Laurie screws Mason jar lids to the bottom of a kitchen shelf so that jars can be filled with snacks and screwed into the lids for creative storage.

181. Gen saves money in Santa Fe: Feliz by covering inexpensive vases and jars with _____.

182. When constructing a fountain that looks like a faux window in Colorado: Berry Avenue, Hildi's plan to waterproof it with silicone doesn't work, and she decides to use _____ instead.

183. Laurie disguises a large-screen television in her mod update of a Colorado: Cherry Street living room by:
- **a.** hanging metallic streamers from the ceiling
- **b.** placing the television behind a partial room screen
- **c.** building tubular steel shelving on either side and above the television
- **d.** slipcovering the entertainment unit in satin

 Answers begin on page 72

184. **For a New York: Half Hollow Turn living room, Frank hangs a custom sculpture in honor of the male homeowner's profession. The sculpture is made from:**
    a. roofing shingles and copper flashing
    b. 2x4s and wood screws
    c. sheet metal and rivets
    d. electrical and plumbing components

185. **In New Orleans: Walter Road, Gen transforms an old rain gutter into a _____.**

186. **In an Alpharetta: Providence Oaks dining room, Hildi adds visual interest to the walls by painting thick horizontal stripes of:**
    a. tinted shellac
    b. translucent glaze
    c. thinned latex paint
    d. opalescent stain

Who designed this room?

Section 4: Answers

1. **B.** "Where your treasure is, there will be your heart"

2. **C.** buying new sofas

3. **B.** place mats and clothespins

4. **D.** candleholders

5. **D.** French tester canopy

6. **dishware**

7. **spatula**

8. **A.** blueprint paper

9. **glass rods**

10. **6**

11. **100**

12. **chinoiserie**

13. **anchors**

14. **place mats**

15. **C.** acrylic

16. **candle sconces**

17. **trombone**

18. **Pharaoh**

19. **A.** pencils

20. **0**

21. **three**

22. **B.** bulletin boards

23. **boiled eggs**

24. **B.** a pair of beer-theme lights

25. **B.** side tables

26. **a leaf**

27. **little wooden houses**

28. **True.** She lays two small black rugs, but the majority of the floor is gray sub-flooring.

29. **True.** The process is messy, but the technique is successful.

30. **A.** window treatments

31. **Christmas lights**

32. **A.** hammers

33. **A.** Paige asks Amy Wynn to return some wood

34. **A.** black-and-white photos of each person's head

35. **False.** She's used the technique only twice—once each in Buckhead: Canter Road and Austin: Wing Road.

36. **True.** Doug's thrifty trick paid off; he ends up under budget.

37. **False.** Doug paints zebra stripes on the walls.

38. **D.** "We are sorry"

39. **A.** a window well liner

40. **D.** bed

41. **C.** skyline

42. **False.** The painting is done on three store-bought canvases and hung as a triptych.

43. **picture frame**

44. **False.** Doug uses the photo to accentuate his Zen Goth design during this episode.

45. **D.** egg whites

46. **her own body parts**

47. **True.** Even with this large expenditure, she still comes in under budget.

48. **zeroes**

49. **dinghy**

50. **holly**

51. **False.** Doug installs the poles in this episode.

52. **pot rack**

53. **India**

54. **False.** She uses the sweaters for throw pillows.

55. **D.** deer

56. **chest**

57. **True.** She previously used the technique on a Seattle: 56th Place living room wall.

58. **pink**

59. **worms**

60. **fish**

61. **C.** a working train track and toy airplanes

62. **A.** beta fish

63. **B.** meat puppets

64. **A.** shampoo chair

65. **C.** cow hides

66. **False.** He installs wooden clouds, complete with raindrops.

67. **A.** radiator covers

68. **A.** monkey

69. **Delta Upsilon**

70. **C.** orange

71. **wooden slipcover**

72. **A.** a barstool

73. **tea bags**

74. **B.** pine

75. **D.** Henri Matisse

76. **False.** She frames Chinese newsprint.

77. **A.** a footstool

78. **baseboards**

79. **C.** wheat and corn

80. **D.** installing a pleated metal screen between the two spaces

81. **True.** The T-shirts happen to be on sale—and in the color Doug wants.

82. **red**

83. **True.** The captain's wheel hung on the wall in the original room design; it complements the sorority's symbol, the anchor.

84. **Venetian plaster**

85. **C.** bowling balls

86. **False.** Gen's team traces Gen's and Paige's silhouettes onto poster board.

87. **A.** "All things are ready if our minds be so"

88. **wire**

89. **C.** eggplants

90. **False.** She wires small tree limbs and twigs onto the fixture.

91. **serape**

92. **valance**

93. **C.** paint the floor black

94. **False.** She makes the table lamp out of an inverted galvanized trash can.

95. **B.** barbecue grill components

96. **B.** ceiling

97. **railroading**

98. **C.** a blowtorch

99. **B.** eliminates the project and leaves the windows bare

100. **ceiling fan**

101. **B.** the homeowners removed the existing wallpaper before he arrived

102. **D.** David loves Noel

103. **C.** basketweave pattern

104. **C.** sewing patterns

105. **crystals**

106. **False.** The place mats have an image of a rose.

107. **A.** basement rec room

108. **6,000**

109. **False.** Gen uses the postcards to decorate the room.

110. **A.** autumn leaves

111. **False.** Gen attempts to drill through rocks but ends up eliminating the project when her drill bit barely scratches the surface.

112. **A.** motorcycle

113. **False.** Vern doesn't have enough money in his budget to purchase the prints, so the kids donate them.

114. **B.** dried leaves

115. **Doug**

116. **False.** Paige is sent to find the household items.

117. **C.** candleholders

118. **False.** While Vern has created the basketwoven fabric and leather headboards (California: Grenadine Way and Missouri: Sunburst Drive, respectively), Doug used the bent tree branches in Orlando: Winterhaven.

119. **D.** Pillow Pods

120. **Slaughterhouse**

121. **B.** wheat grass

122. **Oregon**

123. **False.** Frank paints the musicians during this episode.

124. **C.** multicolor ribbons

125. **False.** Vern uses the frames as cabinet doors during this episode.

126. **C.** malachite

127. **C.** seashells

128. **flowers**

129. **fabric**

130. **cigar boxes**

131. **C.** is too big to fit through the doorway

132. **True.** The treatment gives the ceiling a silver-leaf look.

133. **D.** pearls

134. **C.** pool noodles

135. **D.** picture frames

136. **False.** She paints it brown.

137. **A.** sewing on bamboo place mats

138. **False.** She paints the brick gray and purple and glues broken pieces of glass on it for a mosaic look.

139. **A.** craft fur

140. **embroidery hoop**

141. **candleholder**

142. **C.** light fixtures

143. **True.** His female homeowner painted it.

144. **artificial grass**

145. **C.** stained wood

146. **D.** souvenir spoons

147. **herself**

148. **record album**

149. **False.** While she planned to include a pyramid-shape fountain in the final design, the project leaks and has to be cut late on Day 2.

150. **herself**

151. **True.** She tells her homeowners she wants it to look like it's coming "out of the sea."

152. **throw pillows**

153. **False.** Frank suspends the swing in the bedroom during this episode.

154. **C.** teepee

155. **tri-fold doors**

156. **wine glasses**

157. **False.** Frank makes the pipe candleholders with the help of his female homeowner in this episode.

158. **B.** first-cut

159. **C.** chain link

160. **plaster**

161. **D.** luck and love

162. **A.** orange asterisks

163. **A.** adhesive

164. **beer**

165. **False.** He's used the fruit bowls (Cincinnati: Sturbridge Road) and the candy dishes (Cincinnati: Madison and Forest), but he has yet to use gutter materials.

166. **dragons**

167. True. She seals the boxes shut so the homeowners' children can't eat the art.

168. False. The beanbag sofa created for this episode was Doug's idea.

169. B. dragons

170. lampshades

171. A. doorbell

172. I

173. B. lightly stained 1x2

174. D. throw pillows

175. duck decoys

176. A. cabinets

177. black foam

178. neckties

179. C. rooster

180. False. She installs them to store dry goods, not sugary treats.

181. self-hardening terra-cotta clay

182. pond lining

183. B. placing the television behind a partial room screen

184. D. electrical and plumbing components

185. picture frame

186. B. translucent glaze

Section 4: Photo Identification Answers

Page 49: Kia

Page 52: Hildi

Page 57: Laurie

Page 60: Kia

Page 65: Dez

Page 68: Frank

Page 71: Edward

Section 5:

the

silly

Cowboy Hats

Tattoos

Sea Otters

French Fries

?

This section is dedicated to some of the most unforgettable—and sometimes the strangest—moments in *Trading Spaces* history. Get ready to tease your brain with pure fun.

stuff

I. Paige and Edward find Jeff and George Stoltz the morning of Day 2 in Los Angeles: Seventh Street taking Polaroids of themselves and Beverly Mitchell's:

a. Emmy Award
b. Teen Choice Award
c. Kid's Choice Award
d. Essence Award

2. True or False? Ty plays guitar, Doug plays the sax, and Hildi sings during B-roll footage in Quakertown: Quakers Way.

3. In a Maine: Joseph Drive bedroom, Frank embellishes a basic rocking chair with:

a. rhinestones
b. metallic paints
c. pet collars
d. beaded fringe

4. In Orlando: Whisper Lake, Hildi wants construction work done in her room that is beyond Amy Wynn's comfort level, so she hires a/an:

a. roofer
b. master carpenter
c. plumber
d. electrician

5. True or False? In Scottsdale: Bell Road, Vern suns himself with a metal dustpan.

6. Gen and her team wear boxer shorts on their _____ while redecorating a living room in Austin: Wampton Way.

7. In an Arlington: First Road bedroom, Hildi's male homeowner leaves a note in black marker on the wall that says:

a. "It's been a blast."
b. "They made me do it."
c. "Dude, this room rocks."
d. "Sorry about the walls."

8. True or False? In Austin: Wampton Way B-roll footage, Gen makes herself disappear as a magic trick.

9. In New Orleans: Jacob Street, host Alex makes _____ that resemble Laurie and Hildi.

10. True or False? In Oakland: Webster Street, Hildi eats two pieces of the straw she plans to glue to the walls.

11. To complement his jungle-theme bedroom design in Pennsylvania: Gorski Lane, Doug:
    a. places a stuffed macaw on a wooden perch in the corner of the room
    b. strings a series of shrunken heads above the bed
    c. fashions a valance from faux gorilla fur
    d. hangs a bunch of real bananas from the ceiling

12. Vegas: Carlsbad Caverns originally aired live:
    a. commercials for other TLC shows
    b. B-roll
    c. Designer Chats
    d. Reveals

13. The homeowners in New York: Shore Road are so excited by Gen's design for their sunporch, they dance the:
    a. Mashed Potato
    b. Twist
    c. Monkey
    d. Roger Rabbit

Based on the number of times they have appeared on cast members' heads, cowboy hats are the most common *Trading Spaces* accessory.

14. Hildi, Gen, and _____ imitate the Beatles' *Abbey Road* album cover in London: Garden Flat.

15. When Andy Dick doesn't want to help Ty install carpentry projects into a Los Angeles: Elm Street office, he recruits his:
    a. lawyer
    b. mother
    c. assistant
    d. makeup artist

16. Gen tests the strength of her suspended television shelf in an Austin: Wampton Way living room by dancing on it. Ty and her male homeowner:

a. boo
b. give her dollar bills
c. clap and serenade her
d. climb up and join her

17. True or False? In Indiana: Fieldhurst Lane, Vern and Amy Wynn toss around hay bales as Kia drives a tractor.

18. During her Designer Chat in Austin: Wampton Way, Gen dresses like the girl in the champagne poster she hangs above the room's fireplace by wearing:

a. matching shoes
b. the same dress
c. a similar necklace
d. her hair in the same style

19. In South Carolina: Innisbrook Lane, Frank does an impression of fellow cast mate _____.

20. Jeff Stoltz paints a section of Edward's room screens in Los Angeles: Seventh Street to look like a tombstone that reads:

a. Here Lies My Career after *Trading Spaces*
b. Edward R.I.P.
c. Rest in Paint
d. Ashes to Ashes, Sawdust to Sawdust

21. While wearing costumes and silly wigs in Austin: Wampton Way, Doug performs a magic trick and cuts Ty in half with a:

a. router
b. chain saw
c. cordless drill
d. handsaw

22. In New York: Sherwood Drive, Doug, Vern, and Amy Wynn play a ball toss game at a carnival. _____ wins.

23. True or False? In a Los Angeles: Irving Street living room, Frank finds a note from his homeowner asking him not to use chickens in the design.

24. In an Austin: Aire Libre Drive living room, Kia's male homeowner scavenges the entire home for decorative accessories and returns with only a:

a. plastic tulip
b. latch-hook rug
c. macramé owl wall hanging
d. glitzy Mardi Gras-theme egg

25. While spending time at an old ghost town in Scottsdale: Windrose Avenue, Paige refers to herself as the *Trading Spaces* _____,

26. In a Los Angeles: Springdale Drive dining room, Vern's homeowners attempt to create a positive mood in the room by:

a. burning sage and incense
b. writing inspirational thoughts on the walls in pencil
c. playing dance music
d. bringing a plate of fresh-baked cookies

27. In Philadelphia: Valley Road, Doug jokingly uses _____ as dental floss, but he doesn't advise trying it.

01:41:21.27

Who designed this room?

28. In San Diego: Hermes Avenue, Gen hangs a cow skull above the living room fireplace as an homage to artist:

a. Jasper Johns
b. Georgia O'Keeffe
c. Vincent Van Gogh
d. Paul Cezanne

29. Robin Leech presents _____ 's team with champagne and toasts the room's newfound style in Vegas: Carlsbad Caverns.

30. In the Los Angeles: Seventh Street celebrity episode, the four homeowners who work with Hildi and Edward are all stars of the show:

a. *Touched by an Angel*
b. *Buffy the Vampire Slayer*
c. *Seventh Heaven*
d. *Everybody Loves Raymond*

31. In California: Via Jardin, Laurie holds a small snake, Amy Wynn holds a large lizard, and Vern holds a scorpion as a _____ sits on his shoulder.

32. In Austin: Aire Libre Drive, Kia shares her carpentry plans with Ty by:

a. painting on a small easel
b. handing Ty a stack of napkins with various doodles
c. sketching on Ty's bicep with a marker
d. drawing on the sidewalk with sidewalk chalk

33. When Paige asks Doug what color he painted the ceiling in Vegas: Carlsbad Caverns, he replies "blush" and slaps her _____ to show her the color.

34. In an Orlando: Lake Catherine bedroom, Hildi adds a live yellow canary to the room that she names:

a. Tweety
b. Pretty Girl
c. Hildi
d. Heidi

35. True or False? In Los Angeles: Willoughby Avenue, Doug and Gen get out of a limo while talking on cell phones as Ty sits behind the wheel.

36. For his design in a Quakertown: Quakers Way living room, Doug, Ty, and Paige sneak over to a neighbor's home and "borrow" a:

a. birdbath
b. shrub
c. lawn gnome
d. gazing ball

37. The one room Beverly Mitchell tells George and Jeff Stoltz to stay out of when spending the night in her home in Los Angeles: Seventh Street is:

a. her bedroom
b. her bathroom
c. her basement
d. her garage

38. True or False? When Andy Dick gets paint on his *Trading Spaces* smock and removes it in Los Angeles: Elm Street, Gen tapes his mike to his bare chest.

39. True or False? Ty playfully puts two large French fries in his mouth as if they were walrus tusks in Los Angeles: Elm Street B-roll footage.

40. In Miami: Ten Court, the homeowners swap keys while:

a. swimming in a lake
b. sitting on jet skis
c. sitting in canoes
d. riding in paddle boats

Three *Trading Spaces* cast members have featured members of their families on the show: Doug's brothers and nephews appeared in Scott Airforce Base: Ash Creek; Laurie's newborn son appeared in several episodes; and Gen's mom appeared in Pennsylvania: Tremont Drive.

41. True or False? In Vegas: Smokemont Courts, Edward's female homeowner puts Paige's hand in her armpit to show her how sweaty she is.

42. After posing on a green screen in Houston: Appalachian Trail, Laurie, Doug, and Amy Wynn's heads are superimposed on a shot of:

a. astronauts
b. space aliens
c. cheerleaders
d. punk rockers

43. In Vegas: Smokemont Courts, Laurie and Edward play _____ while Amy Wynn runs the table.

44. In Miami: Miami Place, Laurie reveals her _____ as a sleight-of-hand magic trick.

45. In Pennsylvania: Bryant Court, Laurie's male homeowner wears a black T-shirt under his smock that reads:
a. "My wife made me do it"
b. "I love Laurie"
c. "Hiya, Mom!"
d. "Whose idea was this, anyway?"

46. Frank's homeowners in Scottsdale: Bell Road spend the night between Days I and 2 at a hotel because:
a. there are problems regulating the house's heat
b. the bathroom floods
c. the paint fumes are too strong
d. a neighbor's dog keeps them awake

01:37:41.06

Who designed this room?

47. In Austin: Aire Libre Drive, Ty lets _____ ride him like a horse.

48. In the Orlando: Whisper Lake end credits, Paige is presented with a cake for her:
   a. 100th episode
   b. birthday
   c. wedding anniversary
   d. appearance on *Hollywood Squares*

49. In Vegas: Carlsbad Caverns, Paige discovers comedienne _____ doing the splits and trying to take over her job.

50. Vern redoes a bonus room in an Austin: La Costa Drive celebrity episode for Natalie Maines, the lead singer of:
   a. The Bangles
   b. SheDaisy
   c. The Donnas
   d. The Dixie Chicks

51. True or False? Doug and Hildi dance as the four homeowners play together in their band in California: Peralta Street.

52. In a Florida: Night Owl Lane bedroom, Paige, Edward, Amy Wynn, and Edward's homeowners play Duck, Duck, Goose during the Load Out footage. _____ 's the goose.

53. While at the beach in Miami: Ten Court, Kia and Hildi sit on lounge chairs and Ty serves them drinks, but he accidentally spills them on:
   a. himself
   b. the sand
   c. Hildi
   d. Kia

54. When the two girls see the new ribbon-theme bedroom Laurie designed for them in Boston: Ashfield Street they:
   a. run out crying
   b. hug Paige
   c. wrinkle up their noses
   d. turn cartwheels

55. During Orlando: Whisper Lake B-roll footage, Hildi, Amy Wynn, and Frank have their pictures taken with:

a. Mickey and Minnie
b. Minnie and Pluto
c. Pluto and Goofy
d. Goofy and Mickey

56. True or False? In an Austin: Wampton Way living room, Gen and her team use the male living room homeowner's tube socks to create the wall's faux finish.

57. In Los Angeles: Murietta Avenue, Gen and Amy Wynn watch as Laurie gets:

a. her license renewed
b. a fake *Trading Spaces* tattoo
c. a spiral perm
d. her navel pierced

Even though Paige celebrated her 100th episode in Orlando: Whisper Lake, it was the 99th to air. The extra episode didn't air until the start of the fourth season.

58. In New Orleans: Walter Road, Frank titles his family-friendly design for a kitchen:

a. Make Way for Dining
b. Kids and Cuisine
c. Brunch with the Brady Bunch
d. Beaver Cleaver Meets George Jetson

59. Paige spray-paints dining chairs red in Los Angeles: Murietta Avenue while Gen's male homeowner plays the _____.

60. Hildi pays an electrician _____ in cash to move three switches and an outlet in an Orlando: Whisper Lake living room.

61. While wearing a Pacer jersey in Indiana: River Valley Drive, _____ bounces a basketball off of her head as if it were a soccer ball.

62. When Hildi throws thrift store couch cushions over the balcony into the pool below in Los Angeles: Seventh Street, actress Jessica Biel says Hildi scored _____ points per pillow that hit the water.

63. In Los Angeles: Murietta Avenue, Gen claims people always say they want _____ when they don't know in what style they want to redo their room.

64. True or False? In Missouri: Sunburst Drive, the cast wears monogrammed shirts while bowling. Gen's bowling shoes are a size 10.

65. Penn & Teller make an appearance during Vegas: Carlsbad Caverns and perform a card trick for Amy Wynn using a:
a. chop saw
b. drill
c. hammer
d. tape measure

66. True or False? Edward pitches, Doug bats, and Ty catches while playing baseball in South Carolina: Sherborne Drive.

67. In Pennsylvania: Gorski Lane, Doug and Frank ride four-wheelers through a field as Ty:
a. runs behind them, trying to catch up
b. builds a scarecrow
c. is pulled behind Frank's four-wheeler on a skateboard
d. hoes a row of beans

68. True or False? Hildi's female homeowner in Miami: Miami Place wears Tazmanian Devil slippers throughout the show.

69. In Indiana: Fieldhurst Lane, Doug calls the design for his orange bedroom all the following except:
a. Indian Summer
b. Sunset Harvest
c. Harvest Sunset
d. Golden Harvest

70. In Los Angeles: Seventh Street, Paige, Beverly Mitchell, and Jessica Biel discover that a mattress in another room of the home they are redoing is supported by milk crates filled with:
a. candy wrappers
b. used books
c. clothes
d. fan letters

71. In Los Angeles: Irving Street, Ty says he feels like he's in the TV show _____ because of the unpredictable conditions.

72. Vern leaves with his team on Day 1 in Orlando: Winter Song Drive to go shopping for a _____.

73. True or False? The cast and crew burn a *Trading Spaces* smock during the end credits of Pennsylvania: Cresheim Road to celebrate the end of the season.

74. In Colorado: Berry Avenue, Hildi brushes _____ on the living room walls to show her homeowners the color she's planning to paint the room.

75. During The Reveal, Edward's female homeowner in Vegas: Smokemont Courts opens her eyes and finds Laurie painted her living room _____ — the one color she didn't want.

76. When Frank hears on the morning of Day 2 in San Diego: Duenda Road that his homeowners went to a party down the street the night before, he's upset because:
  a. they invited other party guests over to see the room's progress
  b. they partied until dawn and are exhausted
  c. they didn't finish their homework
  d. he wasn't invited

77. When firemen are checking the kitchen in Miramar: Avenue 164 after a tripped fire alarm, Doug nonchalantly offers them:
  a. a seat
  b. chips
  c. paintbrushes
  d. autographs

78. True or False? Doug and Ty play catch with a baseball in a Scottsdale: Windrose Avenue bedroom as Doug's team arrives.

79. In Los Angeles: Murrieta Avenue, Gen's male homeowner, Teddy, plays guitar and has toured with Alice Cooper, Slash's Snakepit, Guns 'N Roses, and:
  a. Cyndi Lauper
  b. Carole King
  c. Poison
  d. Pearl Jam

Answers begin on page 96

80. When Hildi's team accidentally breaks the legs off a Depression-era piano in a Florida: Night Owl Lane living room, Amy Wynn repairs them by replacing the:

a. dowel rods
b. casters
c. L-brackets
d. wood screws

81. In Indianapolis: Halleck Way, Amy Wynn waves the checkered flag at an Indy car driven by:

a. Gen and Laurie
b. Frank and Vern
c. Kia and Doug
d. Edward and Kia

82. Frank's male homeowner in San Diego: Fairfield bought new shoes to wear on the show, but early on Day 1 he:

a. steps in a full paint tray
b. breaks his foot
c. thinks they're uncomfortable and switches to his old, comfy shoes
d. decides to go barefoot

01:39:20.03

Who designed this room?

83. True or False? For an Indiana: River Valley Drive living room, Gen serves as the model for the large triptych painting of a foot.

84. True or False? In Vegas: Carlsbad Caverns, Hildi and Doug go to a drive-in marriage chapel in a convertible where an Elvis impersonator officiates.

85. At the end of Austin: Wyoming Valley Drive, the neighbors enter a kitchen decorated with hundreds of wine labels and give their friends
   a. a gallon of block-out white paint
   b. a bottle of wine and an apology note
   c. a wallpaper steamer tied with a ribbon
   d. a pair of paint scrapers

86. True or False? Doug takes a break from working on his design for a sunporch in Orlando: Winter Song Drive by sitting in the homeowners' sauna.

87. In Pennsylvania: Tremont Drive, Amy Wynn pushes Gen and Vern around in a:
   a. shopping cart
   b. wheelbarrow
   c. baby stroller
   d. laundry cart

88. In Scottsdale: Bell Road, Frank's homeowners have two birds named _____, one of which relieves itself on Frank's head.

89. When all four homeowners come together at the end of the show in Vegas: Woodmore Court, they drink from extra-large:
   a. beer steins
   b. margarita glasses
   c. martini glasses
   d. coffee mugs

90. Despite the fact that Laurie repeatedly vetoes it, Laurie's homeowners in Miami: 168th/83rd Streets really want to install:
   a. mini-blinds
   b. a wet bar
   c. wallpaper border
   d. a faux fireplace

Answers begin on page 96

91. In a Scottsdale: Windrose Avenue bumper shot, Frank and Doug "duel," pulling _____ from their holsters.

92. When Ty, Frank, and Vern are on a hike in Scottsdale: Bell Road, Vern carries a:
  a. walking stick
  b. map
  c. water bottle
  d. large rock

93. In a Wake Forest: Rodney Bay living room, Laurie and her homeowners spend much of the episode scrubbing a white sofa because:
  a. the sofa is dirty, and Laurie based the room design around it
  b. Paige accidentally spills red paint on it
  c. Amy Wynn accidentally covers the sofa with sawdust and wood shavings
  d. the homeowners' hands are greasy when they move the sofa out of the room

94. In Maryland: Village Green, Doug, Gen, and Amy Wynn take a hayride, and Doug spots:
  a. the Headless Horseman
  b. Nearly Headless Nick
  c. the Great Pumpkin
  d. Bigfoot

95. True or False? In Miramar: Avenue 164, Edward's room is so large that he's spreading bread crumbs through it when he first meets his homeowners so that they can find their way around.

96. In a Chicago: Spaulding Avenue bedroom, Hildi draws large "swooshes" of grass on the walls with chalk pastels and then seals the design with:
  a. shellac
  b. hair spray
  c. clear nail polish
  d. polyurethane

97. When Ty finishes his light carpentry load early in Austin: Aire Libre, he enlists the neighborhood kids to:
  a. play hide and seek with him
  b. wash the *Trading Spaces* trailer
  c. give him a manicure
  d. sweep up the carpentry area

98. In an Austin: Wycliff kitchen, Doug hangs several clocks on the wall without batteries installed because:

    a. he can't afford to buy them
    b. he titles the room Frozen in Time
    c. he purchased the wrong type of batteries
    d. the homeowners can't stand the sound of ticking clocks

99. While handing Doug a drill during Vegas: Carlsbad Caverns, an Elvis impersonator sings _____.

100. Vern arrives the morning of Day 2 in Santa Monica: Ocean Park to find his two young female homeowners have pinned his headshot to their shirts and call themselves the:

    a. Vernierockers
    b. Vernettes
    c. Yippers
    d. Yip Sisters

101. The only thing Hildi brings back into the living room from the original design in Miami: Ten Court is _____.

Who designed this room?

102. True or False? In San Diego: Hermes Avenue, Laurie's homeowners offer to buy a new toaster for their neighbors' kitchen as a gift. Laurie agrees because she's out of money.

> To promote the Vegas: Carlsbad Caverns episode featuring live Reveals, Paige taped a commercial in which she sings, dances, and wears a showgirl costume.

103. In Los Angeles: Elm Street, a celebrity episode, Gen redoes Sarah Rue's office and Vern redoes Andy Dick's kitchen. Sarah and Andy are currently on the show _____.

104. Frank's homeowners don't finish their homework in Key West: Elizabeth Street, claiming that neighbors came over with:
   a. popcorn and videos
   b. cake and ice cream
   c. champagne
   d. nachos

105. There are several shots throughout San Diego: Duenda Road of a SeaWorld seal and sea otter having fun with:
   a. Paige
   b. Frank
   c. Vern
   d. Amy Wynn

106. In a Long Island: Steuben Boulevard great room, Frank makes a large pig-topped weather vane to sit above the fireplace. He names it _____.

107. In Los Angeles: Elm Street, Andy Dick gets _____ on Paige's jeans—on purpose.

108. Gen and Amy Wynn dance on a partially laid bed platform in Pennsylvania: Tremont Drive while humming:
   a. "The Star Spangled Banner"
   b. "You're a Grand Old Flag"
   c. "Stars and Stripes Forever"
   d. "America the Beautiful"

109. True or False? Vern proudly shows off his new tattoo in California: Via Jardin by flexing his right bicep for the camera.

110. True or False? In Austin: Wampton Way, Gen's team removes the existing sectional couch to find a body outline beneath it.

111. Teddy, Gen's male homeowner in Los Angeles: Murietta Avenue, is friends with the guitarist Slash, who stops by the set while Gen and Teddy are:
- **a.** sewing pillows
- **b.** framing photos of 1940s Los Angeles
- **c.** painting the walls dark red
- **d.** installing a new light fixture

112. In Santa Clara: Lafayette Street, Frank adds a festive touch to the living room of a:
- **a.** Chi Omega sorority house
- **b.** Zeta Tau Alpha sorority house
- **c.** Delta Gamma sorority house
- **d.** Alpha Delta Pi sorority house

01:39:28.10

Who designed this room?

113. Gen's male homeowner in Austin: Wampton Way goes to Carpentry World to work with Ty wearing nothing but:
   a. a baseball hat and work gloves
   b. boxer shorts and safety glasses
   c. a tool belt and several strategically placed paint chips
   d. work boots and a drop cloth sarong

114. Doug's male homeowner calls him _____ for no apparent reason in Austin: Wampton Way.

115. Paige lets _____ call Time's Up in South Carolina: Innisbrook Lane.

116. In a Colorado: Stoneflower Drive bedroom, Frank fools his homeowners into believing that his design will include:
   a. dolphin pillows
   b. lava lamps
   c. inflatable furniture
   d. a bubble machine

117. In Austin: Wampton Way, Doug plays _____ on a bumper shot.

118. Ty chases Doug and Kia in a motorized cart customized to look like an _____ in Scott Airforce Base: Ash Creek.

119. The coffee table Gen builds in a San Diego: Hermes Avenue living room features legs made of:
   a. antique porch banisters
   b. firewood
   c. PVC pipe
   d. cardboard packing tubes

Section 5: Answers

1. **B.** Teen Choice Award

2. **False.** Hildi doesn't croon any tunes— she plays the drums.

3. **C.** pet collars

4. **D.** electrician

5. **False.** Ty uses the dustpan to get a tan during this episode.

6. **heads**

7. **B.** "They made me do it."

8. **False.** Paige pulls off the magical feat in this episode.

9. **voodoo dolls**

10. **False.** Paige eats the straw during The Reveal.

11. **D.** hangs a bunch of real bananas from the ceiling

12. **D.** Reveals

13. **C.** Monkey

14. **Handy Andy**

15. **C.** assistant

16. **B.** give her dollar bills

17. **False.** Doug drives the tractor.

18. **B.** the same dress

19. **Laurie**

20. **B.** Edward R.I.P.

21. **B.** chain saw

22. **Amy Wynn**

23. **False.** The homeowner asks Frank not to use any sheep.

24. **D.** glitzy Mardi Gras–theme egg

25. **sheriff**

26. **B.** writing inspirational thoughts on the walls in pencil

27. **picture wire**

28. **B.** Georgia O'Keeffe

29. **Doug**

30. **C.** *Seventh Heaven*

31. **spider**

32. **D.** drawing on the sidewalk with sidewalk chalk

33. **cheeks**

34. **C.** Hildi

35. **False.** Ty is riding in the trunk—and talking on a cell phone.

36. **D.** gazing ball

37. **A.** her bedroom

38. **True.** Andy then strikes poses for the camera.

39. **False.** Gen gives herself tusks; Ty jokingly puts one up his nose.

40. **C.** sitting in canoes

41. **True.** She wants to prove she's not goofing off.

42. **A.** astronauts

43. **roulette**

44. **fabric swatch**

45. **D.** "Whose idea was this, anyway?"

46. **A.** there are problems regulating the house's heat

47. **Paige**

48. **A.** 100th episode

49. **Rita Rudner**

50. **D.** The Dixie Chicks

51. **True.** There's a lot of hip bumping!

52. **Amy Wynn**

53. **D.** Kia

54. **D.** turn cartwheels

55. **B.** Minnie and Pluto

56. **False.** The trio uses the homeowner's boxer shorts to dab at the paint.

57. **B.** a fake *Trading Spaces* tattoo

58. **D.** Beaver Cleaver Meets George Jetson

59. **accordion**

60. **$100**

61. **Gen**

62. **10**

63. **French country**

64. **False.** She bowls barefoot.

65. **B.** drill

66. **False.** Carter catches, not Ty.

67. **C.** is pulled behind Frank's four-wheeler on a skateboard

68. **False.** Her yellow slippers have Tweety Bird's face on them.

69. **A.** Indian Summer

70. **C.** clothes

71. *M*A*S*H*

72. **sectional sofa**

73. **False.** They roast the cream Season III pillow that appeared in every episode.

74. **melted chocolate**

75. **brown**

76. **D.** he wasn't invited

77. **B.** chips

78. **False.** They're tossing a football. Ty even leaps to catch a pass and falls on the bed.

79. **B.** Carole King

80. **A.** dowel rods

81. **D.** Edward and Kia

82. **A.** steps in a full paint tray

83. **False.** Doug is the foot model for the artwork in this episode.

84. **False.** Amy Wynn pronounces the "couple" man and wife.

85. **C.** a wallpaper steamer tied with a ribbon

86. **False.** He takes a dip in the hot tub.

87. **A.** shopping cart

88. **Cinnamon and Yoko**

89. **C.** martini glasses

90. **D.** a faux fireplace

91. **paintbrushes**

92. **D.** large rock

93. **A.** the sofa is dirty, and Laurie based the room design around it

94. **C.** the Great Pumpkin

95. **False.** Frank spreads the bread crumbs through a large bedroom during the episode.

96. **B.** hair spray

97. **B.** wash the *Trading Spaces* trailer

98. **A.** he can't afford to buy them

99. **"Amazing Paint"**

100. **B.** Vernettes

101. **a Pluto toy**

102. **False.** The neighbors purchase new hardware as a gift for their neighbors.

103. *Less Than Perfect*

104. **C.** champagne

105. **D.** Amy Wynn

106. **Poopalina**

107. **primer**

108. **C.** "Stars and Stripes Forever"

109. **False.** He does sport what looks like a tattoo on his bicep, but it's never mentioned and it isn't there in his next *Trading Spaces* appearance.

110. **True.** It was left as a joke by the homeowners.

111. **A.** sewing pillows

112. **C.** Delta Gamma sorority house

113. **C.** a tool belt and several strategically placed paint chips

114. **Sparky**

115. **fans**

116. **A.** dolphin pillows

117. **trombone**

118. **airplane**

119. **B.** firewood

Section 5: Photo Identification Answers

Page 81: Vern

Page 84: Edward

Page 89: Roderick

Page 92: Gen

Page 94: Frank

"Linoleum bites."
"No table dances until February."

the
Section 6:
qu

?

Although many of the words of wisdom offered by the *Trading Spaces* cast may not be recited decades from now, these quotable quotes are just plain fun.

otes

"oh la la, my room rocks!"

"I'm not a one designer kind of guy."

1. Who is Laurie's female homeowner referring to when she says, "I think she already understands that we don't want anything on the wall except paint."

2. Who does Frank call "My little wood nymph!"
   a. Ty
   b. Amy Wynn
   c. Carter
   d. Paige

3. When a salesman tells Laurie, "We're gonna make it in your price range," in Los Angeles: Murietta Avenue, what is she shopping for?

4. What causes Kia to cheerfully say, "That's better than $100," to Paige in Pennsylvania: Cresheim Road?

5. Who said: "I thought ... country quilt. This looks like a quilt threw up in here, but when you see the result, you're gonna love it."

6. What prompts one of Hildi's homeowners to exclaim in Mississippi: Winsmere Way, "It's raining panties!"

7. Who said: "You can't spend money to buy time."

8. Which designer is reminded by a homeowner, "It's okay not to be happy sometimes."

9. Who said: "[The measurement is] one fat man with arms extended."

10. Who said: "If you can protect our country, you can hang moss."

11. What does a homeowner in Los Angeles: Irving Street ask Frank not to include in his room that prompts him to say, "There goes my whole damned design."
    a. chickens
    b. sheep
    c. faux finishes
    d. copper eye wall sculptures

12. What is Laurie referring to in Santa Monica: Ocean Park when she tells Paige, "This is supposed to evoke question."

13. Who said: "It's a lot like some people. They're just very showy but they're totally not functional."

14. Who is a female homeowner referring to when she says, "Well, now he's a little cranky."

15. What are Frank and his team doing when he says, "There is less choreography in *Swan Lake*," in Maine: Joseph Drive?

16. Who said: "It's like Olé! Olé! and we're not into that right now."

17. Who said: "There are no mistakes. There are just embellishment opportunities."

18. What is a South Carolina: Innisbrook Lane homeowner touching when he says, "I'm gonna get a jogging suit just like this!"

19. Who said: "With people dying everywhere and starving children, really, two ceiling fans of the wrong color are minor trivialities."

20. When Laurie says in New Jersey: Tall Pines Drive, "Can I just, like, blink and click my heels and this'll be done," what project is she concerned about?

21. Who said: "The Slipcover Queen comes to the rescue."

22. To whom does Ty exclaim, "You've switched out folk for funk!"

23. What is Gen's team doing in San Diego: Elm Ridge that prompts Amy Wynn to ask Alex, "Are they trying to prove they can make a bedroom look like a patio?"

"I want to give them a room that is a basic skeleton with beautiful walls, the layout the way I think it needs to be ... and then, hopefully, what I trigger them to do [is buy new furniture]." Laurie, Chicago: Edward Road

24. What type of computer software does Gen describe to Paige in Colorado: Berry Avenue, by saying, "[It's a] special program for a special girl."

25. Who said: "To me, a bedroom is supposed to have a lot of pillows."

26. Who said: "I had a kid walk by and throw a coin in my mouth and make a wish."

27. Who said: "Welcome to the fraternity!"

28. What is Gen referring to when she tells her homeowners in Pennsylvania: Tremont Drive, "It's not gonna come in in bunches but in subtle punches."

29. Who said: "I know you think that we just have a hot glue gun and some chintz fabric, but that's not the case."

30. Who said: "We're gonna make a metal taco."

31. Who said: "Am I showing too much cleavage? Be honest."

32. Who said: "Everything in this room is gonna be very Zen, very sleek. Clean, minimal lines."

33. Which cast member is Gen's female homeowner referring to when she says, "[He's] easy on the eyes."
a. Doug
b. Edward
c. Vern
d. Carter

34. To whom does actor Andy Dick say, "When you look good, I look good."

35. Who said: "My powers of perception go beyond simple rotation!"

36. Who is Frank talking about when he tells his homeowners, "He goes through like life's little pixie, like a gnome looking for a mushroom."

37. When Frank says, "It's like bad reception, it goes in and out" in Key West: Elizabeth Street, what is he referring to?

38. When a male homeowner sees his newly redecorated room in South Carolina: Innisbrook Lane and exclaims, "Who cares about the table? We got 10 lemons out of the deal," where are the lemons?

39. Who said: "I'm gonna take a quick five."

40. Who is Frank impersonating when he says, "She'd call it something like Amber Cream or Buttermilk Fawn."

41. Who said: "Oh, by the way, you're gonna be up all night and it's gonna be a lot of work. Welcome to *Trading Spaces*."

42. What is one of Gen's male homeowners referring to when he says, "[It] smells like somebody's old underwear," in San Diego: Elm Ridge?

43. Who said: "No more celebrity episodes!"

44. Who said: "I will take you by the hand, lead you to the river of paint, and dip you in it and baptize you to the great religion of faux finishes."

45. Whom did Hildi advise to: "Delegate, delegate, delegate."

46. Who said: "Jedi costumes equal slipcovers to me."

Who designed this room?

47. What is Doug talking about in Orlando: Winter Song Drive when he tells his homeowners, "It's gonna stay. I'm a giver."

a. the sofa
b. a beer light hung over the bar
c. the existing ceiling fan
d. the carpeting

> "Precision doesn't have to go overtime. You just have to be well planned." Vern, Maryland: Fairway Court

48. Who said: "[Romance] doesn't have to be, like, socko-wow leather and lace."

a. Frank
b. Gen
c. Paige
d. Edward

49. Who said: "Did they know who was coming to dinner?"

50. What decorative element is Frank talking about when he tells Paige, "I just can't leave without some funky little nonsensical nerdy thing like that," in New York: Linda Court?

51. Who said: "If I see one more howling coyote wearing a bandanna, so help me, I'm gonna run amok."

52. What is Laurie describing in Mississippi: Winsmere Way when she exclaims, "[It's] disco '70s nightmare!"

a. her homeowner's shoes
b. the shade of purple paint she intended to use in the room
c. the mirrored ball that hangs in the room
d. the existing upholstery

53. To whom does Frank say, "You're gonna have to change from total professional to sleaze ball."

54. Who said: "I like giving life to things that would be discarded."

55. What is Vern referring to in Wake Forest: Rodney Bay when he tells Paige, "This is not a viable, workable solution."

56. Which cast member is Gen describing when she says, "[He's] all show, no go."
a. Carter
b. Ty
c. Handy Andy
d. Doug

57. Which cast member is Hildi's male homeowner joking about when he says, "He is just the looks behind the show and not the brains!"

58. What new item is a female homeowner excited about in Virginia: Gentle Heights Court when she sees Kia's finished design and says, "I wanna jump in there and get naked!"

59. Who said: "I want to give them a room that has, like most relationships or marriages, some whimsy, some peacefulness, and a little bit of tactile sensitivity and sexuality."

60. Who said: "I'm getting this surge of power from [being] over budget."
a. Frank
b. Edward
c. Laurie
d. Vern

"I think it's important whenever you do something that's remotely hip ... that you are able to update. Otherwise you're stuck in something that becomes very passé." Gen, Los Angeles: Willoughby Avenue

61. Who said: "When you're working with a $1,000 budget, you've got to faux it up a bit."

62. Who said: "Because that's all we are on this show—a bunch of professionals."
a. Doug
b. Gen
c. Amy Wynn
d. Paige

63. Who said: "Ooh la la, my room rocks!"

64. Who said: "This is driving me crazy right now that this isn't going on in a straight line."

65. Who said: "I'm so tense...you could literally use me as a paper press."

66. Who said: "Art stands alone."
   a. Edward
   b. Vern
   c. Laurie
   d. Gen

67. What design element is Paige referring to in Indianapolis: Halleck Way when she asks Kia, "So, homeowners beware?"

68. Who said: "I sound bad but I am so perky."

69. Which designer does a homeowner assure, "When I get married I will never pull up carpet, ever!"

Who designed this room?

70. When Laurie says, "I cannot in good faith do this room and not do this," in **Wake Forest: Rodney Bay,** what is she referring to?

    a. slipcovering the couch
    b. removing the existing ceiling fan
    c. painting the fireplace yellow
    d. scattering vases filled with lemons throughout the room

71. Who said: "I'm so happy because I'm on America's No. 1 torture show."

    a. Ty
    b. Doug
    c. Vern
    d. Frank

72. Who said: "Black is so appetizing."

73. Who said: "Tin is not a two-day project, just so you know."

74. On what does an **Orlando: Whisper Lake** homeowner write a note to Frank reading, "I love your work. I only hope I still do on Friday."

75. Who said: "You're looking at the winner of the date with Mary Poppins' Look-a-Like Contest."

    a. Ty
    b. Hildi
    c. Paige
    d. Frank

76. Who said: "Yeah, Laurie is known for neon."

77. Who said: "I may have just had a panic attack over nothing."

78. What is Gen surprised to see in **Vegas: Woodmore Court,** prompting her to say, "Now that's good craft fun!"

79. Who said: "Every Southern woman needs a chaise longue."

80. Who said: "Anarchy, baby!"

    a. Hildi
    b. Amy Wynn
    c. Paige
    d. Kia

81. Who does Frank describe as, "very tall, very gorgeous, and has enough sex appeal to knock over a troupe."

82. Who said: "The second day is the one to really sweat."

83. Whom does Frank ask, "Are you sure you aren't a reincarnated 2-year-old?"

84. Who said: "You could get malaria in this room it's so tropical."

85. What is a male homeowner asking about when he sees Doug's living room design in Indiana: River Valley Drive and says, "What is that? An olive?"

86. Who said: "It's so hard getting used to all these different people's houses, you have no idea."
   a. Paige
   b. Amy Wynn
   c. Edward
   d. Laurie

87. Who said: "You'd better get some popcorn and a good attitude because this is something you wanna write home to your mother about."

88. Who said: "That's, like, the Spam of wood."

89. Who said: "If you were in Pompeii just before Vesuvius erupted and you grabbed a piece of furniture, it would be this table."
   a. Amy Wynn
   b. Frank
   c. Laurie
   d. Vern

90. Which designer is Gen talking about when she says, "He might have a lot of attitude but he's a damn fine designer."

91. Who said: "My body's in the way of the entire wall!"

92. Who said: "If you're so damned secure, start putting that stuffing in that pillow."

93. Which spiky-haired cast member does Hildi kid by saying, "Look who's talking, porcupine!"

94. What item is Frank telling his homeowners about in Long Island: Steuben Boulevard when he says, "I pitched such a wall-eyed fit about not having one in plastic that they gave me a 10-percent discount."

  a. a framed print
  b. a rug he purchased to lay in the living room
  c. an upholstered chair
  d. a small decorative statue

95. What is Frank talking about in Boston: Institute Road when he says, "It could be the gates of heaven or the portals of hell."

  a. what could be under the carpet he's about to remove
  b. what he'll find under the couch cushions
  c. what will be in the attic when he goes to look for decorative items
  d. what will be in the shipping package he just received

96. Who said: "You've annoyed me enough now."

97. What is Doug in the middle of when he tells his female homeowner, "There's no way you're gonna stop me, so don't even try," in Pennsylvania: Gorski Lane?

98. Who said: "When God created the world, I was out there painting a fence."

> "I always think you need a touch of black in a room." Edward, Missouri: Sweetbriar Lane

99. Who said: "*Trading Spaces*, where everything seems to go wrong."

100. What is Gen doing in a Colorado: Cherry Street living room when she warns, "Don't do this if you're renting."

101. Who said: "It's Tracee?! Oh my gosh, I've been calling her Stacey the whole time!"

102. What is Doug doing in Vegas: Carlsbad Caverns when Hildi tells him, "Stop opening your mouth!"

  a. eating fried chicken
  b. talking
  c. kissing her
  d. checking his teeth

103. Who said: "OK, I'll work this in between my tennis match with the Royal Family and my tanning appointment."

104. When Laurie's homeowners in Mississippi: Winsmere Way say, "They don't show the real life crap," what are they having difficulty doing?

105. Who said: "Try and get the feeling of what it would be like if you were a dog and you were laying in your bed going, 'I need a little wall decor here.'"

> "[Try] redecorating by relocating." Kia, Austin: Aire Libre Drive

106. What happened to a wall in a Miami: Miami Place living room that Hildi and her team have to repair, causing her to say, "This is way beyond our call of duty."

107. Who said: "Those birds are gonna be the end of me."

108. Which cast member does Gen tell, "I would fear your baby nuggets!"
   a. Ty
   b. Doug
   c. Amy Wynn
   d. Paige

109. Who is Gen describing when she says, "He's an attitude carpenter. It's all business out here."

110. Who said: "Everyone in America knows I can rip up that carpet if I want to."

111. Who said: "All of a sudden I feel like I have to go out and buy a dress for the prom because I do this all the time."

112. Which cast member is Gen talking about when she says, "I think he's feeling insecure about his room or he's got a little crush on me and he's just really sad about the rejection."

113. When Frank tells Paige in Providence: Wallis Avenue, "The squealing is gonna be like the Chicago stockyards when they see that," what is he talking about?

114. Who said: "No table dances until February."

115. Who said: "[I'm] in a panic mode."

116. What is Kia looking at her reflection in when she tells Paige, "I'm a little distorted and very prismed," in San Diego: Fairfield?

   a. a piece of broken glass
   b. a metal pizza pan
   c. a sheet of metal flashing
   d. a CD that she wants to use to make a mirror

117. Who said: "We like smiley faces on people but no smiley faces on walls."

118. What is Frank distressing for a Colorado: Andes Way living room when he tells his team, "The kids are gonna beat this up, so it might as well look that way already."

   a. the fireplace surround
   b. a kid's art table
   c. the coffee table
   d. the slipcovered sofa

Who designed this room?

119. Who is Gen's female homeowner referring to when she says, "He hasn't been a real jerk yet."

120. Who said: "Some days it goes quickly. Some days it just doesn't."

121. Who said: "Chocolate brown is my absolute favorite color."
   a. Edward
   b. Paige
   c. Doug
   d. Laurie

122. Who said: "Linoleum bites."

123. What is Doug referring to when he tells Paige in Arlington: First Road, "It's growing on her like a fungus, but it's growing."

124. Who said: "I've done 30-some *Trading Spaces* episodes. I know what... I'm doing."
   a. Ty
   b. Kia
   c. Hildi
   d. Doug

125. Who said: "I don't know what that Broom-Hilda was doing over there."

126. Who said: "What are we going to do to rip this room to shreds for two days and have a good time doing it?"

127. Which of Gen's projects in Colorado: Cherry Street prompts Amy Wynn to say, "Wow. That's scary looking."

128. What element of Doug's design is he referring to in New Jersey: Lincroft when he tells his homeowners, "It's not as obnoxious as it could be."
   a. the animal stripes he painted around the room
   b. the several different accent colors he uses in a living room
   c. the gazing ball statue he built
   d. his ceiling paint choice

129. Who said: "Prepare yourselves for the final squeal."

130. Who does Frank warn, "As cute and precious as you are, some of you are not going to make it back into this room."

131. Who said: "If someone invited me out to dinner I'd have to hire someone to chew my food."

132. What is Doug doing when he says to his Orlando: Whisper Lake homeowners, "Shhh! I'm trying to plan."

133. What is Frank talking about in Missouri: Sweetbriar Lane when he tells Paige, "During the Civil War I used to make 'em for the troops."
  a. slipcovered tents
  b. uniforms
  c. sashes
  d. crinolines

134. Who said: "Only serious professionals need to apply to this job!"

135. Who said: "Why did we even come here [if they don't want us to change things]?"

136. What are Frank and Alex making in Knoxville: Stubbs Bluff when he tells her, "Make it look like you just went to the jungle and knocked over a monkey and dug up the soil and put it on a pot."

137. Which designer is a homeowner speaking to when he asks, "People go over budget on movies every day! Why can't you go over budget on a couch?"

138. Who said: "As a nurse you should know ... never leave a sponge in anything."

139. Who said: "Oh my God, shoe storage! I love it!"

140. Who said: "[*Trading Spaces* is] a game of risk and jeopardy."

141. Who said: "I want this to be the pit of wild monkey love."

142. Who said: "Become one with your batting."

143. What is Ty describing when he tells Edward in Long Island: Steuben Boulevard, "It looks like Vegas!"

144. To whom does Gen say, "You can go naked or you can wear that shirt."

145. Who said: "[I'm in a] slo-mo hot zone."

146. Who said: "I think it's important to streamline and clean up rooms as much as possible."

"Most craft projects can be done with stuff found around the yard." Frank, Colorado: Cherry Street

147. Who said: "I mean, how serious can you get with a potato?"

148. What is Doug talking about in Miramar: Avenue 164 when he asks his homeowners, "Have people not learned that these are not good taste?"
- **a.** skorts
- **b.** macramé owls
- **c.** refrigerator magnets
- **d.** garden gnomes

TCR 01:40:31:05

Who designed this room?

149. Which of Hildi's designs does her male homeowner describe to Amy Wynn by saying, "It's gonna be like a death room."

150. Who said: "Let me write that down so I can embroider that on a whoopee cushion."

151. Who said: "If I can handle power tools, I can handle you."
   a. Amy Wynn
   b. Gen
   c. Paige
   d. Laurie

152. Who said: "This means that my absolute plan is foiled."

153. What material are Frank and one of his female homeowners giggling about in Maine: Joseph Drive when he says, "They come in all sizes, just as in life."

154. Who said: "I'm not a one designer kind of guy."

155. What does Hildi's female homeowner describe to Paige as "a big egg yolk" in Pennsylvania: Bryant Court?

"Every room has to have a little quirk in it." Doug, Austin: Wampton Way

156. Who said: "Isn't it just like life? You work and you work and you work and ... a bird poops on you."

157. What is Doug referring to in Seattle: 137th Street when he tells Ty, "This may be my shining moment."

158. Which designer is told by a homeowner, "You guys love cloth!"
   a. Laurie
   b. Vern
   c. Edward
   d. Doug

159. Who said: "This is a pretty unappetizing, relatively unappealing, vulgar yellow."

160. Which cast member is Frank talking about when he says, "The compassion of a speed bump."

161. Who said: "I can't continue to educate people on what's good taste."

162. What is Frank referring to in Miramar: Avenue 164 when he tells Paige, "It's bigger than my town."

163. To whom does Frank say, "I just brought you a bench and you've given me a piece of sculpture."

164. Who said: "It can't be a man tool if a woman has to show a man how to do it."

165. Who said: "I'm a 5-year-old kid with chest hair."

166. Who said: "[Architects] get all the women."

167. What is Carter referring to in South Carolina: Innisbrook Lane when he tells Laurie's male homeowner, "Back in the day, boy, we didn't have this kinda stuff."

168. What element of Edward's design in a South Carolina: Sherborne Drive living room causes his male homeowner to joke, "Seriously, Edward, this makes me feel a lot better about my home improvement projects."
   a. covering the walls in tissue paper
   b. gluing fabric gimp on the walls as crown molding
   c. hanging a rug on the wall
   d. sawing a custom metal sculpture

169. Who said: "I think it's always nice whenever you're going to change something in someone's house to leave something vaguely familiar so it's not going to be dramatic but there's something comforting as well."

170. Which cast member is Doug's male homeowner impersonating when he says, "Look at my cute little Sandy Duncan hair!"

171. Who said: "To me that's what this room is all about. The remarkable story of the maple and the wood and the whole journey to get to this finished product."

172. Who said: "[The design's] gotta hold up for 30 minutes; then we'll be outta town."
   a. Kia
   b. Doug
   c. Hildi
   d. Frank

173. What does Ty find behind a bookcase in a Miami: Miami Place living room that prompts him to say, "I lost this one in '83!"

174. Who said: "If this were a country it would be Beigeland."

175. Who said: "How many times have you told yourself, 'I wish I weren't here. I wish I was out sewing somewhere'?"

176. What does Frank ask Amy Wynn to make for him in Athens: County Road when he says, "Give me a 4-year-old heiny width."

177. Who said: "I have a college degree. Reduced to a beaver."
   a. Doug
   b. Frank
   c. Ty
   d. Vern

178. Who said: "No one has time for Escher today."

179. Who said: "It's very *Trading Spaces* for this not to work and [for] us to have another hour of work."
   a. Carter
   b. Gen
   c. Frank
   d. Edward

180. Which designer does a homeowner ask, "So you're gonna take his $5,000 bed and replace it with this?"

181. To whom does Gen admit, "You do have ... a little shanty town going here."

182. Who said: "Throw me on the ground and make me write a bad check."

183. What element of Doug's den design in South Carolina: Sherborne Drive prompts Paige to say, "It's a dust trap!"

184. Which designer's homeowner tells him/her, "You could've lived in pioneer times."

185. What is Amy Wynn holding in her mouth when she warns, "Don't do this at home," in Vegas: Woodmore Court?
   a. nails
   b. drill bits
   c. allen wrenches
   d. staples

186. What is Frank doing when he exclaims, "Hey, there's a note from Christopher Columbus under here!" in Texas: Sherwood Street?

187. Who said: "This is a show of human errors."

188. Who said: "What can you do with a box and a magazine rack? I mean, even Vern, my God, even Vern couldn't do anything with that!"

189. When a cheerleading squad coached by a homeowner stops by, whom do they cheer for by chanting, "Fix that space. You're an ace."
   a. Gen
   b. Doug
   c. Vern
   d. Laurie

190. Who said: "Do you like clean lines and straight things? Vern does."

191. Who said: "I've been around the hambone more than once."

192. Who said: "I don't do ugly."

193. Who is Frank referring to when he says, "I just love the way she says, 'You know, I think this will be just perfect here, don't you?'"

194. Who said: "If somebody tells me that a designer is just this little guy who goes around fluffing flowers, I intend to break every bone in their body and make a lamp out of him."

195. Who is a male homeowner talking about when he tells Paige, "If I were in charge she wouldn't get away with this."
   a. Hildi
   b. Kia
   c. Gen
   d. Laurie

196. When Doug tells his homeowners, "We don't want to give her 'old lady'" in Knoxville: Forest Glen, what is the offending item?

197. Which piece of furniture in Frank's New Jersey: Perth Road living room does he describe by saying, "It's kind of a puppet theater cathedral."

198. Which designer does a homeowner kid, "I wish you spent as much time laying this out as you did on your hair this morning."

199. Who said: "I found these lights that, you know, light up."

200. Who said: "I feel like someone's given me a wad of chewing gum and said, 'Go fill up the Grand Canyon.'"

Who designed this room?

201. To whom does Gen say, "I don't care what show you're on. You're doin' some homework."
 a. Andy Dick
 b. Beverly Mitchell
 c. Sarah Rue
 d. Alyson Hannigan

202. Who said: "What's the heiny quotient on that?"

203. What is Gen planning to redo when she tells her team, "We're gonna turn this into a rusty delight," in Los Angeles: Elm Street?

204. Who said: "I try to show people different things to do with the obvious."
 a. Hildi
 b. Kia
 c. Vern
 d. Gen

205. What item in Frank's Boston: Institute Road living room does he say would exclaim, "I'm going to mold you to death!" if it could talk?

206. Who said: "This is real life. This is not page 47."

207. Who said: "I've never used a slipcover before."
 a. Hildi
 b. Paige
 c. Carter
 d. Kia

208. Who said: "Every little girl needs a monkey in her room."

209. Who said: "We're going to be doing a kind of rectangular, kind of check-ique, not really country, not really contemporary, just homey, cottagey, but with a kind of a more upbeat level."

210. Who said: "You are wed."

211. Who said: "If this [bedroom design] doesn't produce a third child, this is gonna be a total failure."

212. Who said: "I can see the beauty in many things."

213. What element in a Berkeley: Prospect Street sorority chapter room does Gen describe by saying, "[It's like] the lobby at the women's clinic."
   a. the carpet
   b. the wallpaper
   c. the furniture upholstery
   d. the existing art

214. Which of Doug's room designs does Paige call "a marvelous achievement."
   a. his China blue chinoiserie mural bedroom
   b. his Art Deco-theater living room
   c. his Pullman car bedroom design
   d. his Jungle Boogie bedroom

215. Who said: "[I want to give people] cleaner spaces and cleaner lines."

"I usually try to find the biggest or the boldest thing that is going to make the most dramatic change." Hildi, New Jersey: Sam Street

216. What is Frank describing in Providence: Wallis Avenue when he says, "[It looks] like a pumpkin threw up in here."

217. What is actress Sara Rue looking at when she tells Paige, "[It's] a garbage can kind of gray," in Los Angeles: Elm Street?

218. Who said: "What's that 'No paint zone' mean to you?"

219. What is Vern's female homeowner looking at in San Diego: Duenda Road when she says, "[It's] like a science project."
   a. dirt under the existing couch
   b. his hair
   c. his detailed drawings of his fireplace tile design
   d. Amy Wynn's carpentry project

220. To whom does Paige say, "You can take a look if you want, but, really, it's just because we're idiots."

Section 6: Answers

1. Hildi, Miami: Miami Place

2. **B.** Amy Wynn, Orlando: Whisper Lake

3. A rug that she goes to purchase late on Day 2

4. Learning she is $79 over budget

5. Frank, Alexandria: Riefton Court

6. Hildi, throwing handfuls of underwear into the air when she realizes a dresser she wanted to refinish hadn't been emptied

7. Paige, San Diego: Duenda Road

8. Doug, Seattle: 137th Street

9. Frank, New Orleans: Walter Road

10. Gen, San Diego: Elm Ridge

11. **B.** sheep

12. Her black and white Gottlieb-inspired art pieces

13. Frank, New York: Linda Court

14. Doug, Seattle: 137th Street

15. Hanging his plastic envelope art piece

16. Gen, Los Angeles: Irving Street

17. **B.** Frank, New York: Linda Court

18. Laurie's ultrasuede sofa slipcover

19 Frank, Knoxville: Courtney Oak

20. The Matisse-inspired mural she paints in a basement rec room

21. Hildi, San Antonio: Ghostbridge

22. Frank, Miramar: Avenue 164

23. Laying outdoor tile as bedroom flooring with liquid adhesive

24. A photo imaging program she uses to enlarge and crop photos

25. Frank, Scottsdale: Windrose Avenue

26. Frank, Providence: Wallis Avenue

27. Hildi, Los Angeles: Seventh Street

28. Bright orange paint

29. Gen, Los Angeles: Elm Street

30. Frank, San Diego: Wilbur Street

31. Frank, Knoxville: Stubbs Bluff

32. Vern, Scottsdale: Bell Road

33. **A.** Doug, Maine: George Road

34. His assistant, Los Angeles: Elm Street

35. Vern, Vegas: Woodmore Court

36. Ty, Knoxville: Stubbs Bluff

37. The shifting control between himself and his male homeowner

38. In a vase above the armoire

39. Actor Andy Dick, Los Angeles: Elm Street

40. Laurie, South Carolina: Innisbrook Lane

41. Paige, California: Via Jardin

42. The Oregon moss Gen plans to hang on the wall

43. Gen, Los Angeles: Elm Street

44. Frank, Texas: Sherwood Street

45. Dez, Lawrenceville: Pine Lane

46. Gen, Austin: Wampton Way

47. **C.** the existing ceiling fan

48. **A.** Frank, San Diego: Fairfield

49. Hildi, Pennsylvania: Bryant Court

50. Wall art that he created to look like gondolier hats

51. Frank, Oregon: Alsea Court

52. **B.** the shade of purple paint she intended to use in the room

53. Ty, Knoxville: Stubbs Bluff

54. Frank, Northampton: James Avenue

55. A dresser Amy Wynn reconstructed on which the drawers won't open

56. **C.** Handy Andy, London: Garden Flat

57. Ty, Miami: Ten Court

58. The bed suspended from the ceiling by chains

59. Frank, Colorado: Stoneflower Drive

60. **A.** Frank, Los Angeles: Irving Street

61. Gen, Philadelphia: 22nd Street

62. **B.** Gen, Missouri: Sunburst Drive

63. Gen, San Diego: Dusty Trail

64. Vern, Orlando: Winter Song Drive

65. Frank, Annapolis: Fox Hollow

66. **C.** Laurie, Santa Monica: Ocean Park

67. Kia's pyramid fountain

68. Frank, Texas: Sutton Court

69. Doug, New York: Sherwood Drive

70. **B.** removing the existing ceiling fan

71. **C.** Vern, California: Via Jardin

72. Paige, Pennsylvania: Bryant Court

73. Gen, San Diego: Dusty Trail

74. His headshot

75. **D.** Frank, Los Angeles: Irving Street

76. Paige, Austin: Wyoming Valley Drive

77. Laurie, Santa Monica: Ocean Park

78. Her male homeowner mooning her through one of the room's windows

79. Laurie, Mississippi: Winsmere Way

80. **B.** Amy Wynn, Florida: Night Owl Lane

81. Gen, Alexandria: Riefton Court

82. Frank, San Diego: Duenda Road

83. Alex, Athens: County Road

84. Frank, San Diego: Wilbur Street

85. The flowers painted on the wall using a stencil Doug designed

86. **B.** Amy Wynn, San Diego: Duenda Road

87. Frank, Orlando: Gotha Furlong

88. Gen, Pennsylvania: Tremont Drive

89. **B.** Frank, Ft. Lauderdale: 59th Street

90. Doug, San Diego: Dusty Trail

91. Frank, San Diego: Duenda Road

92. Frank, New Jersey: Perth Road

93. Ty, Orlando: Lake Catherine

94. **B.** a rug he purchased to lay in the living room

95. **A.** what could be under the carpet he's about to remove

96. Handy Andy, London: Garden Flat

97. Painting large zebra stripes across all four walls of a bedroom

98. Frank, Providence: Wallis Avenue

99. Gen, Pennsylvania: Tremont Drive

100. Cutting a large rectangle in the middle of the existing wall-to-wall carpet in order to create an inlaid rug

101. Paige, South Carolina: Innisbrook Lane

102. C. kissing her

103. Frank, Northampton: James Avenue

104. Hanging a towel rack

105. Frank, Colorado: Stoneflower Drive

106. Water damage

107. Paige, Scottsdale: Bell Road

108. A. Ty, San Diego: Dusty Trail

109. Handy Andy, London: Garden Flat

110. Hildi, Plano: Shady Valley Road

111. Frank, Philadelphia: Gettysburg Lane

112. Doug, Cincinnati: Sturbridge Road

113. The dishwasher he bought for his homeowners

114. Hildi, Ft. Lauderdale: 59th Street

115. Laurie, Maple Glen: Fiedler Road

116. D. a CD that she wants to use to make a mirror

117. Frank, Scottsdale: Bell Road

118. B. a kid's art table

119. Doug, Maine: George Road

120. Ty, Missouri: Sunburst Drive

121. A. Edward, Florida: Night Owl Lane

122. Gen, Buckhead: Canter Road

123. His female homeowner's feelings on his bedroom design

124. D. Doug, Arlington: First Road

125. Doug, Knoxville: Forest Glen

126. Frank, Seattle: 137th Street

127. Gen's inlaid carpet project

128. B. the several different accent colors he uses in a living room

129. Frank, Pennsylvania: Gorski Lane

130. The stuffed animals in a girl's bedroom, Scottsdale: Bell Road

131. Frank, San Diego: Wilbur Street

132. Sitting in a hot tub

133. D. crinolines

134. Gen, New Jersey: Catania Court

135. Doug, New Jersey: Lincroft

136. Creating moss-covered flowerpots

137. Frank, Los Angeles: Irving Street

138. Frank, New York: Half Hollow Turn

139. Amy Wynn, San Diego: Duenda Road

140. Laurie, Pennsylvania: Bryant Court

141. Frank, Maine: Joseph Drive

142. Frank, San Diego: Fairfield

143. Edward's bed design that includes lights under the bed frame

144. Actor Andy Dick, Los Angeles: Elm Street

145. Gen, Maple Glen: Fiedler Road

146. **Roderick, Alpharetta: Providence Oaks**

147. **Frank, Austin: Birdhouse Drive**

148. **C.** refrigerator magnets

149. **Her Pennsylvania: Bryant Court dining room. She paints the walls and ceiling black**

150. **Frank, New York: Linda Court**

151. **B.** Gen, Maine: George Road

152. **Laurie, Vegas: Smokemont Courts**

153. **Pipe nipples**

154. **Ty, San Diego: Dusty Trail**

155. **The yellow oval dining table**

156. **Frank, Scottsdale: Bell Road**

157. **His plan to build a wooden slipcover for a fireplace instead of painting it**

158. **D.** Doug, Seattle: 137th Street

159. **Paige, Pennsylvania: Bryant Court**

160. **Doug, Pennsylvania: Gorski Lane**

161. **Doug, Arlington: First Road**

162. **The size of the bedroom he's redecorating**

163. **Amy Wynn, Providence: Wallis Avenue**

164. **Amy Wynn, Pennsylvania: Tremont Drive**

165. **Frank, Athens: County Road**

166. **Vern, New Orleans: D'evereaux Street**

167. **Having so many toys as a child that you needed something large to store them in**

168. **A.** covering the walls in tissue paper

169. **Gen: Alexandria: Riefton Court**

170. **Paige, Los Angeles: Willoughby Avenue**

171. **Vern, Scottsdale: Bell Road**

172. **D.** Frank, Austin: Birdhouse Drive

173. **A cassette tape**

174. **Gen, Colorado: Cherry Street**

175. **Frank, Scottsdale: Windrose Avenue**

176. **A wooden swing he plans to hang from the ceiling of a girl's bedroom**

177. **B.** Frank, New Jersey: Perth Road

178. **Gen, Washington, D.C.: Quebec Place**

179. **B.** Gen, Vegas: Woodmore Court

180. **Vern, Santa Monica: Ocean Park**

181. **Ty, Los Angeles: Irving Street**

182. **Frank, Boston: Institute Road**

183. **The draped poster board ceiling**

184. **Hildi, Athens: County Road**

185. **A.** nails

186. **Removing what appears to be very old wallpaper**

187. **Gen, Seattle: 56th Place**

188. **Frank, Los Angeles: Irving Street**

189. **B.** Doug, Houston: Appalachian Trail

190. **Gen, Missouri: Sunburst Drive**

191. **Frank, Providence: Wallis Avenue**

192. **Edward, Florida: Night Owl Lane**

193. **Laurie, South Carolina: Innisbrook Lane**

194. **Frank, New Orleans: Water Road**

195. **B.** Kia, San Diego: Fairfield

196. **Unused fabric his team finds around the house and wants him to incorporate in the design**

197. **An armoire**

198. **Doug, Washington, D.C.: Cleveland Park**

199. **Hildi, Pennsylvania: Cresheim Road**

200. **Frank, New Orleans: Walter Road**

201. **A.** Andy Dick, Los Angeles: Elm Street

202. **Frank, Annapolis: Fox Hollow**

203. **A filing cabinet; she plans to oxidize the surface with a special paint technique**

204. **A.** Hildi, Austin: Wyoming Valley Drive

205. **The carpet**

206. **Frank, Providence: Wallis Avenue**

207. **D.** Kia, Scott Air Force Base: Ash Creek

208. **Frank, Scottsdale: Bell Road**

209. **Frank, Seattle: 137th Street**

210. **Amy Wynn, Vegas: Carlsbad Caverns**

211. **Vern, California: Corte Rosa**

212. **Hildi, Mississippi: Winsmere Way**

213. **D.** the existing art

214. **C.** his Pullman car bedroom design in Maryland: Fairway Court

215. **Vern, Orlando: Lake Catherine**

216. **The existing orange linoleum kitchen floor**

217. **The paint color Gen used in her office**

218. **Amy Wynn, Orlando: Smith Street**

219. **C.** his detailed drawings of his fireplace tile design

220. **Firemen who show up at Doug's room because of a tripped fire alarm, Miramar: Avenue 164**

Section 6: Photo Identification Answers

Page 103: Doug

Page 106: Kia

Page 111: Hildi

Page 114: Laurie

Page 119: Gen